I WAS A SLAVE™

True Life Stories Dictated by Former American Slaves in the 1930's

Book 5: THE LIVES OF SLAVE CHILDREN

Compiled by
Donna Wyant Howell

Cover Photograph:
Children Dancing in Front of
Southern Slave Cabin
(Names Unknown)

AMERICAN LEGACY™ Books • Washington, DC

The **I WAS A SLAVE**™ Book Collection

AMERICAN LEGACY™ **Books**

Library of Congress Catalog Card Number: 98-73931

ISBN 1-886766-12-6

Copyright © 1998 Donna Wyant Howell
First edition copyright © 1997 Donna Wyant Howell

Published in the U.S.A.
Publisher:
American Legacy Books
Washington, DC

First revised edition, first printing, 1998
(First edition, 1997)

All rights are reserved. No part of this book may be reproduced, entered into a retrieval system, nor transmitted in any form by any means, whether electronic, mechanical, photographic, photocopying, manual (by hand), digital, video or audio recording, or otherwise; nor be produced as a derivative work; nor be included on the internet (except for mentions of the books); nor be performed publicly in any manner without the prior written consent of the copyright owner. To request consent, write to or call Donna Wyant Howell at the address or telephone number below. Explain the nature of the proposed usage and include address and daytime telephone number. Most requests are granted.

Photographs are courtesy of the Library of Congress except on page 4 and wherever else indicated.
The versions of the photographs contained in this book are the property of the above named copyright owner.

Charitable organizations, please ask for our **Fundraising Brochure** by writing to: American Legacy, P.O. Box 1393, Washington, DC 20013 or call 202-737-7827. The Donna Wyant Howell Speaking Brochure also is available.

Contents

Important Information 5

Terminology 7

Dialect Glossary 9

The Lives of Slave Children 11

    General Descriptions 12
    Housing 14
    The Plantation Nursery 18
    Food 24
    Clothing 27
    Playtime 30
    Work 33
    The Slave Children and the Slaveowner's Children 44
    Childhood Remembrances 46

Full Life Stories

    Allen Sims 49
    Eda Rains 51
    Isaac Martin 53
    Lily Perry 61

List of Subtitles of Books 63

The **I WAS A SLAVE** Book Collection
is dedicated to the millions* of enslaved people whose toil helped to create America

Cora Wyant and her children

and to my great-grandmother
CORA WYANT
1856-1963
who first stirred my interest when I was nine
by telling me about that wonderful day when she was nine
when she and her mother held hands
as they walked off the plantation
— *FREE!*

and to all the descendents of African slaves,
as well as African American freeborns
(including my maternal freeborn ancestors)
who suffered indirectly due to the institution of slavery

and to the millions of my brothers and sisters
who today still bear much weight.

(*estimated total transported from Africa and born into slavery: over 60 million from 1565 to 1865)

Important Information

This book is one in the series of The I WAS A SLAVE™ Book Collection. It contains excerpts and full interviews revealing the true life stories of former American slaves — **as told by the ex-slaves themselves.** Interviewers working for the Work Projects Administration transcribed thousands of pages of these dialogues which now are housed in about six archival repositories throughout the United States. The former slaves ranged in age from their early seventies to well over one hundred years.

These interviews occurred during the late 1930's, a time of great economic depression in the United States. This depression affected everyone, especially America's poorest citizens, among whom were some of these formerly enslaved people. For many of those who had been treated humanely, remembrances of youthful days resurfaced with desires to return to times when food was plentiful. Those who had been abused knew that even the worst depression was a far better way of life.

SILVIA KING: Oh, I jes' can' 'member all dem good things us had in dem days. Sho' wish us had 'em now.

JENNY PROCTOR: Ise hear tell of dem good slave days but I ain't nev'r seen no good times den.

DONAVILLE BROUSSARD: I don't know whether it's been better since the war. I don't mean slavery was better than to be free. I mean times were better.

You will notice that the structure and spellings vary widely. While a few former slaves had gone on to attain college degrees, most remained almost, if not completely, illiterate. The skills of the writers conducting the interviews also ranged from excellent to barely adequate. Most of the slaves spoke like the uneducated Southern whites from whom they learned their speech patterns. Indeed, many whites, including some of the slaveowners themselves, were barely literate. A small number of slaves, especially the house slaves of well-educated whites, spoke grammatically correct English. Thus, it is difficult to determine if and when minor or extensive editing was done by the interviewers. Additionally, many were edited numerous times, creating several versions of the same dialogue. Other interviewers faithfully wrote their spellings of Southern dialect for every single word as pronounced by the ex-slaves.

Remember that discrimination and persecution were flourishing openly during the time of these interviews. The various attitudes directed towards these freed blacks by the interviewers — who were male and female, black and white — also affected the responses. (Most were white women.) Nevertheless, the majority of the ex-slaves were as candid as they dared to be and told significant amounts of details about their days in slavery.

CATO CARTER: Everythin' I tell you am the truth, but they's plenty I can't tell you.

As instructed to do, most writers followed the supplied questionnaire and queried their interviewees about a long list of topics, including ones such as their masters', parents', and siblings' names; treatment; work; food; and ghost stories. Others ignored the questionnaire procedure and let the ex-slaves have a free-flow conversation about any number of subjects.

As I compiled these precious words, I dared not do any extensive editing. I present them to you essentially as the interviewers wrote them, whether that was in dialect writing or in edited writing. Keep in mind that these writers often created several versions. I made very minor changes, such as correcting obvious typographical errors and adding or deleting *some* of the commas. I have included bits of information to you that I have enclosed [in brackets]. The interviewers' comments are enclosed (in parenthesis).

I am so pleased to present the following true life stories. Through them, we are able to learn much oral American history while enjoying the delicious Southern flavor of the words with which many of the slaves expressed themselves.

Blessings to you,

Donna

Terminology

plantation = a large farming estate cultivated by workers producing crops and products for market

master or mistress = male or female slaveowner

quarters = slaves' cabins where they slept and sometimes ate

overseer = the person, almost always a white man, who had the duty of ensuring that the slaves completed all of their tasks, and of punishing the slaves (if allowed to do so by the owner); the overseer was hired by the owner, was a relative of the owner, was a slave of the owner, or was the slaveowner him or herself

pattyrollers, patterollers, patters = patrollers = white men, usually on horseback, who were hired by neighboring groups of slaveowners to patrol the areas surrounding the slaveowners' plantations at any time, but especially at night; the patrollers were paid to catch and whip slaves who were off their respective plantations without a written permission slip which was called a "pass"

pass = a permission slip, written by a slave's owner or overseer, which was required to be carried at all times by a slave when traveling anywhere not on the slaveowner's property; being caught without a pass could result in severe whippings or other punishments

potliquor, pot likker = liquid from food cooked in water, such as collard greens' liquid, making a flavorful and nutritious broth

half, halves, on the half or ha'f, shares = sharecropping = the sharing of the profits of farming; after Emancipation, some ex-slaveowners offered to supply the land and, if agreed, the ex-slaves supplied the labor to raise crops; the two shared the profits, usually 50% each, but sometimes the ex-slaves received only a third, or were deceived and received nothing

suit = a set or outfit of clothes; not a "suit" as the word is used currently; for slaves, this usually consisted of homespun clothing: a dress for women, pants and a shirt for men, and a dress (also called a shirt or shirttail) for both male and female children

slip = a straight dress; not underwear as the word is used currently

nigger = a term used during the time of slavery which referred to a slave or to a free black person and was used by both blacks and whites with little or no animosity (there were exceptions); currently used as an extremely derogatory and inflammatory term (there are exceptions)

nigger driver = a male slave who was the assistant to the overseer or performed the job instead of the overseer; also known as the overlooker

nigger trader = **slave trader** = almost exclusively, a white man whose business was buying, selling, trading, and often breeding slaves

refugeeing = fleeing to the West, usually to Texas, where slaves were taken by their owners who believed that there, in that state, they still could keep their slaves even if the Confederacy lost the Civil War

Juneteenth = June 19th = the name coined by former slaves meaning June 19, 1865, the date of the first time that many slaves were told of their freedom (which officially was proclaimed in the Emancipation Proclamation issued by President Abraham Lincoln in September 1862, which became effective on January 1, 1863); celebrated by ex-slaves yearly, beginning in 1866, as "Emancipation Day" in a few places, primarily in Texas; now observed nationally as an annual holiday with festivities by African Americans and many others

Ku Klux Klan = Klux, Klu Klux, Kluxers, Klan, KKK = an organization initially composed of Southern white males; members frequently wore white robes and hoods over their entire heads to conceal their identities; usually traveled by horseback at night; terrorized blacks, whites who were sympathetic to blacks, and others; terrorized by means of verbal and psychological abuse, beatings, whippings, destruction of property, human burnings, lynchings (hangings), and other forms of murder

hire out = the renting of slaves by their owners to other people to work for a day, month, year, or any period of time; the slave sometimes lived with the other person during the rental period

servant = a term often used to denote a slave who worked in or around the slaveowner's house, such as the cook, maid, butler, coachman, and other house slaves who were frequently (but not always) clothed, fed, and housed a little better than the field slaves

dinner = lunch **supper** = dinner

Dialect Glossary

ALSO SEE PAGES 7 AND 8

I have not tried to create a complete dialect glossary. It contains only the words most frequently used in this book series. Apostrophes vary widely. — *Donna*

ain't = am not, is not, are not, do (does, did) not, have (has) not, etc.
allers, allus = always
allus = all of us
atter = after
aw = all
ax = ask, asked
better'n = better than
brudder = brother
'cause, 'cose, 'caze, case = because
chillun, chillen = children
chap = child
clo's, close = clothes
'cose, corse, course = of course
cotch = catch, caught
cullud = colored
cum = come
dar = there
darsn't = dare not
dat = that
dawg = dog
day = they, their (sometimes day means day)
de = the
dem = them, those
den = then, than
dere, deir = their, there
dese = these
dey = they, their, there
dis = this
'do, do' = although; though; door
dose = those
effen = if
'em = them, him
en, en' = and
eny = any
er = a, an
er = or
et = ate
fer = for, far

fit = fought (sometimes fit means fit)
fo'ks = folks
froo = through
fur's = as far as
fust = first
Gawd = God
gib = give, gave
git = get
goobers = peanuts
gwine = going
hab = have
hafter = have to
hawg = hog
hit = it (sometimes hit means hit)
hoss = horse
iffen = if
Ise = I
Ise, I'se, I's, Ize = (I is) I am, I was, (I has) I have, etc.
jes', jis', jus' = just
jine, jin' = join
kaize, kaise = because
ketch = catch, caught
kin = can (sometimes kin means kin)
Kluxers = Ku Klux Klan (page 8)
lak = like
'lasses = molasses
Lawd = Lord
li'l = little
'lowed = said, declared; allowed
mai'ies = marry, marries
mammy = mother; also the title of the head house slave
Marster, marse, massa = master
mek = make, makes, made
Missus, missy, ol' miss, mistus = mistress
mo' = more
nigh = near
'nuff = enough

9

nuss = nursemaid; caregiver for children and the elderly (a <u>wet</u> nurse breastfed both black and white babies)
ob = of
onliest = only
pappy = father
patterrollers, pattyrollers, patters, patrolas = patrollers (page 7)
pickanninny, picanninney = a slave baby or toddler
plum = all; completely
po', pore = poor
quatahs = quarters = slaves' cabins
rations = food
sar = sir
sarbant, serbent = servant = house slave
sech, sich = such
set = sit, sat
sho, sho' = sure
slap = completely; all the way (sometimes slap means slap)
soon's = as soon as
sont = sent
sot = sat, set (sometimes sent)
suh = sir
sumpin' = something
'tain't = it is not, there are not, etc.
'taters = potatoes
ter = to
thar = there; their
they = their, there (sometimes they means they)
'tell, 'til = until

tote = carry
'twarn't = it was not, there were not, etc.
'twix, 'twixt = between
'twon't = it will not, there will not, etc.
tudder, tother, todder = the other
tuk = took
ub, uv = of
ud = would
udder, odder = other
uh = a, an
'um = him, them
us'n, us's = us, we, our
uster = used to
vittles, vittels = victuals = food
wah = war
warn't = was not, were not
w'en, wen = when
weuns, we'uns = we, us, our
whar = where
wid = with
w'ite, wite = white
wo'k, wuck, wuk, wukk = work
wuz = was, were
y'all, yawl = you all (the plural of you)
yas = yes
yes'm, yes'um = yes madam
yo' = you, your
younguns = children
yous, youse = you, your
yuh = you, your
'zactly = exactly

An apostrophe (') indicates that one or more letters are missing from a word:

buildin's = buildings
he'p = help

can' = can't
'lect = recollect

f'om = from
fo' = for

-ah = -er or -r when used at the end of a word:

fouah = four
heah = hear

ordah = order
flooah = floor

powah = power
buttah = butter

Please READ "Important Information" on pages 5 and 6 FIRST.

THE LIVES OF SLAVE CHILDREN
— Excerpts from Full Life Stories —

You frequently will notice that one person gives some information immediately followed by <u>another person who says the exact opposite.</u> Both can be correct since there was no standard or "average" plantation. Each plantation was as different as its owner.

*The following photographs are of **real** slave cabins and other items from the time of slavery. Photographs have been chosen to show examples of items described by interviewees but are not necessarily the same items used by the interviewees.*

PLEASE UNDERSTAND:
I'm continuously locating photographs, many of which never have been published. There is not an abundance of photographs of slaves and only a few of the ex-slaves had their photos taken during the interviews in the 1930's. As a result, some of the <u>same photographs</u> are repeated in different books. — Donna

GENERAL DESCRIPTIONS

Children's names unknown

SALLIE PAUL: Some of the colored people fared good en' some of dem fared bad in slavery time. Some of dem had good owners en' some of dem had bad ones. Thank de Lord, I didn' get much of it 'cause I won' but nine years old when freedom come.

PAULINE GRICE: De plantation was a big one, ovah 150 grown slaves, an' 'twas 'bout 50 picanninneys [slave babies and toddlers], an' 'bout de same numbah younguns [older children] dat jus' ready to start to wo'k.

BEN CHAMBERS: De chillen allus [always] b'long to dey mama's marster.

AGNES JAMES: I know 'bout Old Miss used to love to feed us, my mercy! She would give us everyone a spoonful of dis here worm cure. Miss would give us all a spoonful of dat every mornin'

General Descriptions

en' den she would ax [ask] us de next mornin' if any us had any worms. Just give us dat en' den feed us some milk en' bread. Dat all she give us.

WILL DAILY: I seen some slaves sold off dat big auction block and de little chillun sho' would be a-cryin' when dey takes deir mothers away from dem.

JOSIE BROWN: I seed some bad sight in slavery, but ain' never been 'bused myself. I seed chillun too li'l to walk from dey mammies sol' right off de block in Woodville. Dey was sol' jus' like calfs.

ADELINE MARSHALL: Don't know nothin' 'bout myself 'cept on Cap'n Brevard's place down on Oyster Creek. He says I's a South Car'lina nigger what he bought back dere and brung to Texas when I jes' a baby. I reckon it de truth 'cause I ain't never knowed no mama or papa, neither one.

SILVIA CHISOLM: I wuz mindin' de overseer's chillun. Mr. Beestinger was his name an' him wife, Miss Carrie. I been eight year old when dey took me. Took me from my mother an' father here on de Pipe Creek place down to Black Swamp. Went down forty-two mile to de overseer! I never see my mother or my father anymore. Not 'til after freedom. An' when I come back den, I been married.

HILLIARD YELLERDAY: When a girl became a woman, she was required to go to a man and become a mother. Master would sometimes go and get a large hale hearty Negro man from some other plantation to go to his Negro women. He would ask the other master to let this man come over to his place to go to his slave girls. A slave girl was expected to have children as soon as she became a woman. Some of them had children at the age of twelve and thirteen years old.

RYER EMMANUEL: My white folks was proud of dey niggers. When dey used to have company to de Big House, Miss Ross would bring dem to de door to show dem us chillun. En [And], My Blessed, de yard would be black wid us chillun all string up [lined up] dere next [to] de doorstep lookin' up in dey eyes. Old Missus would say, "Ain' I got a pretty crop of little niggers comin' on?" De lady, she look so please like. Den Miss Ross say, "Do my little niggers want some bread to gnaw on?" En' us chillun say, "Yes'um, yes'um, we do." Den she would go in de pantry en' see could she find some cook' bread to hand us. She had a heap of fine little niggers, too, 'cause de yard would be black wid all different sizes. Won' none of dem big enough to do nothin'.

CATO CARTER: They [There] was money tied up in li'l nigger young'uns.

SALLIE PAUL: I remember dey would give us chillun all de milk en' hominy [a corn product] us could eat 'twixt [between] meals. Always fed de nigger chillun to de white folks' yard 'twixt meals. You see, dey was mighty particular 'bout how dey would raise en' feed de little niggers in dem days. Would keep dey little belly stuff' wid plenty hominy en' milk, same as dey was pigs. Dey do dat to make dem hurry en' grow 'cause dey would want to hurry en' increase dey property. De white folks never didn' despise [always liked] to see a big crop of nigger chillun comin' on.

WILLIE WILLIAMS: De Marster lots ob times looks dem over an' points one out an' says, "Dat one will be wo'th a thousan' dollahs" an' he points to anudder an' says, "Dat one will be a whopper". Yous see, 'twas jus' lak raisin' de mules. If yous don' hurts dem w'en deys am young, yous gits good strong niggers w'en deys am big.

HOUSING

Some children lived in the slaveowner's house:

SOLBERT BUTLER: Massa take me as a little boy as a pet. Took me right in de carriage! Had a little bed right by his own an' take care of me.

Housing

BUD JONES: I growed up in the house of Old Master. He had a big, log house. I slep' in a little side room built on the Big House. I had a carpet on the floor to sleep on and one to cover up with. It was a fine, good enough bed in warm weather, but I used to near freeze to death when it was cold.

Slave cabins made of planks in Alabama
For more information and photos of different types of cabins, see **Chapter 1**.

THOMAS COLE: My sister's name was Sarah and my brother's name was Ben. We lived in one room of the Big House, and allus had a good bed to sleep in and good things to eat at the same table, after de white folks gits through.

JERRY BOYKINS: When I was young, I lived right in de Big House with my marster. I was houseboy. I slept on a pallet [quilts or other bedding on the floor] in de kitchen. In wintertime on cold nights, I 'members how cold I would get. I'd wake up and slip in my marster's bed. Den I'd say, "Marster John, I's about to freeze." He'd say, "You ought to freeze, you little black devil. What you standin' dere for?" I'd say, "Please, Marster John, jes' let me crawl in by your feet." He'd say, "Well, I will dis one time," and dat's de way I'd do every cold night.

MINTIE MARIA MILLER: He [The slaveowner] had two girls an' I use'

I WAS A SLAVE

to sleep on de foot of deir bed. Dey was nice to me. Dey spoil me in fack.

ANNIE OSBORNE: Me and my brother Frank slep' in Missy Bias' house on a pallet. No matter how cold it was, we slep' on that pallet without no cover, in front the fireplace.

But most of the children lived in the slave quarters:

PETER MITCHELL: Mammy was de housegal. In summer, she kep' us chillen near de Big House in de yard, but we couldn't go in de house. In winter, we stays 'round de shack where we lives while mammy work.

ROSIE McGILLERY: Our quarters in South Carolina were built out of logs with the cracks stobbed with mud, so's we would not freeze in cold weather.

ANNE BROOME: Us live in a two-room plank house.

ANNE MADDOX: Our houses was lak horse stables, made of logs wid mud an' sticks dobbed in de cracks. Dey had no floors. Dere warn't no furniture 'cept a box fer de dresser wid a piece of looking glass [mirror] to look in. Us had to sleep on shuck [cornshuck] mattresses an' us cooked on big fireplaces wid long hooks out over de fire to hang pots on to bile [boil].

ELLEN BUTLER: Us used to live in a li'l log cabin house with one room. The floor was dirt and the house was make jus' like they used to make 'tater [potato storage] house. They was a little window [usually a square hole with no glass] in the back. They jus' have a old frame with planks to sleep on and no mattress or nothin'. In winter, they have to keep the fire goin' all night to keep from freezin'. They put a old quilt down on the floor for the li'l folks.

MARY SELLERS: We had rope beds with shucks in the ticks for mattresses and plenty of cover to cover up with in cold weather.

GEORGE HENDERSON: The cabin I was born in had four rooms,

Housing

two above and two below. The rooms above were called lofts, and we climbed up a ladder to get to these rooms. We slept on trundle beds, which were covered with straw ticks [mattresses]. Our covers were made in big patches from old cast-off clothes. When we got up in the morning, we shoved the trundle bed back under the big bed.

JOHN SNEED: Mos' and usual, de chillen slept on de floor, unless with de old folks. De bedsteads make of pieces of split logs fasten with wooden pegs and rope criss-cross. De mattress make of shucks tear into strips with maybe a li'l cotton or prairie hay. You could go out on de prairie [in Texas] 'mos' any time and get 'nough grass to make de bed, and dry it 'fore it put in de tick. De white folks have bought beds haul' by ox teams from Austin and feather beds.

GEORGE STRICKLAND: Us quarters had dirt flo's [floors] an' was in two long rows wid a street between. On de east side of de settlemunt was de barns, shops, an' sich like. De beds was boxed up an' nailed to de wall, den dey was filled wid pinestraw. Dey fed us li'l niggers [children] in wood troughs made of poplar. De cook in de Big House cooked pots of greens an' po'd potlikker [poured liquid from cooked greens] an' all in de troughs. Us et hit [We ate it] wid mussel shells or wid us's han's or gourds.

Children's names unknown; photograph circa Emancipation

THE PLANTATION NURSERY

On many plantations, infants and small children were cared for in a cabin that was set aside for that purpose:

JULIA MALONE: Ise 'membahs dat Ise left in de nursery by my mammy while [she] am wo'kin' in de field.

RYER EMMANUEL: Oh, dey had a old woman in de yard to de house to stay dere en' mind all de plantation chillun 'til night come, while dey parents was workin'. Dey would let de chillun go home wid dey mammy to spend de night. Den she would have to march dem right back to de yard de next mornin'. We didn't do nothin' but play 'bout de yard dere en' eat what de woman feed us. Yes'um, dey would carry us dere when de women would be gwine to work. Be dere 'fore sunrise. Would give us three meals a day 'cause de old woman always give us supper 'fore us mammy come out de field dat evenin'. Dem bigger ones, dey would give dem clabber en' boil peas en' collards sometimes. Would give de little babies boil pea soup en' gruel en' suck bottle. Yes, ma'm, de old woman had to mind all de yearlin' chillun en' de babies, too. Dat all her business was. I recollects her name. It been Lettie. Would string [line up] us little wooden bowls on de floor in a long row en' us would get down dere en' drink just like us was pigs. Oh, she would give us a iron spoon to taste wid, but us wouldn' never want it. Oh, my Lord, I remember just as good. When we would see dem bowls of hot ration, dis one en' dat one would holler, "Dat mine, dat mine." Us would just squat dere en' blow en' blow 'cause we wouldn' have no mind to drink it while it was hot. Den we would want it to last a long time, too. My, I can see myself settin' dere now coolin' dem vittles.

ANDY J. ANDERSON: De plantation have 12 families of slaves. Thar am 'bout 30 ol' an' young wo'kers, an' 'bout 20 picaninnies dat am too young fo' wo'k. Dem dat am too young fo' wo'k am tuks care of by a nurse durin' de day while de mammies am a-wo'kin' in de field an' sich.

GUS FEASTER: On all de plantations, dar was old womens too old to do any work. Dey would take and study what to do fer de ailments of grown folks and li'l chilluns. Fer de li'l chilluns and babies, dey would take and chaw [chew] up pine needles and den spit it in de li'l chillun's mouths and make dem swallow. Den when dey was a-teachin' de babies to eat, dey done de food de very same way.

Dem babies was washed every day. If dey mammies was in de field, dat never made no diffuns kaise it was de old ladies' jobs to see to it dat dey was. Younguns on de plantations was bathed two or three times a week. Mullin leaves and salt was biled [boiled] in great big pot to put in de babies' wash water and also in de chilluns' water. Dis would keep 'em from gitting sick. Den dey was allus greased atter [after] de washing to keep de skins from busting open. Mos'ly dey was greased wid tallow from de mutton [sheep].

<u>Mothers on some plantations had permission to return to the nursery or to have their babies brought to them during the day:</u>

ANDREW GOODMAN: The mammies was give time off from the

fields to come back to the nursin' home to suck [breastfeed] the babies.

ANK BISHOP: All de women on Lady Liza's place had to go to de fiel' ev'y day. Dem what had suckerlin' babies would come in 'bout nine o'clock in de mawnin' an' when de bell ring at twelve an' suckerlin' 'em. One woman tended to all of 'em in one house. Her name was Ellie Larkin an' dey call her "Mammy Larkin". She all time sarnt [sent] me down in de fiel' for to git 'em come suckle de chillen 'caze dat made hit [it] hard on her when dey gets hongry an' cry.

HENRY BROWN: At one o'clock, the babies were taken to the field to be nursed, then they were brought back until the mothers finished their work, then they would come for them.

Mothers on other plantations were not allowed to see their children until their daytime work was completed:

STEVE ROBERTSON: W'en dis old nigger am de picaninny, Ise 'membahs dat Ise lives in de nursery all de week long. Yous know, weuns don't see our mammy 'cept on Sunday mo'nin'. Deys wo'k diffe'nt places on de plantation all de day long. W'en deys comes in aftah dahk, weuns am all 'sleep. Deys only 'lowed to tooks de sucklin' babes out wid dem.

JEPTHA CHOICE: Until they was about three years old, they wasn't 'lowed 'round the quarters, but was wet nursed [breastfed] by women who didn't work in the field and kept in separate quarters. In the evenin', their mammies were let [allowed] to see 'em.

CLARA BRIM: Dey uster had one ol' lady to cook for all de han's and one to ten' to de chilluns. Dey was a big bunch of dem chilluns, dey sho' was. Dey had a nuss woman what would give de li'l ones breas' nuss [would breastfeed the children] when dey mammies was out wukkin'.

JESSIE PAULS: W'en me am baby, my mammy wo'ks in de field durin' de day, an' gits me f'om de nursery at night w'en she comes in

The Plantation Nursery

aftah suppah. Aftah me big 'nough fo' to feed widout my mammy, me eats wid de res' of de kids. Weuns have wood plates, but tin spoons an' cups fo' de coffee. Co'se, de coffee am coffee-flavored milk wid sugah, but 'twas good an' weuns lapped it right up. 'Twas a fight 'twix [between] weuns kids evah time Nurse Judy Sneed turn her back. Her name am Sneed 'cause she am bo'n on de plantation b'longin' to de Sneeds. All de nigger slaves dat am bo'n on de plantations tooks de name of de ownah. Well, Judy am in hahd place 'cause she love weuns an' don't want weuns hurt, but she have de o'dahs to 'po't [report] to Mistez Rindy w'en de troublements comes up 'twix weuns. Mistez Rindy do de lickin' [spanking] herself. Most de time w'en de kids gits a lickin', she heahs de racket [noise] an' comes a-flyin'. She don't wait around but grabs me first, an' pounds de whey outer me [spanked me very, very hard], den grabs tudder kids. Dat's de way 'twas. Me first, den de res'. She say w'en she gits me, she know she done got part of de troublement.

HENRY BROWN: The old woman and young colored girls who were big enough to lift them took care of them.

PAULINE GRICE: She have help. 'Twas several of de young gals dat 'sist her.

ANTHONY CHRISTOPHER: I know all I did was watch de ones what was littler'n me while de mammys was workin'.

ELLEN POLK: I had to feed de children while deir mudders was in de fields. Missy Hannah would have de cooks fix de grub in a big pan and I would take it to de cullud quarters and feed 'em.

A.C. PRUITT: One old, old lady what am 'mos' too old to git 'round, she take care de chillen and cook deir food sep'rate. She take big black iron washpots and cook dem plumb full of victuals [food]. Come five in de evenin', us have de bigges' meal.

JIM HENRY: Dere was so many, twenty-five or thirty, dat they had to be fed out of doors. At sundown, they was 'sembled in a tent, and deir mammies would come and git them and take them home. Dere used to be some scrappin' [arguing] over de potliquor dat was brought out in big pans. De little chillun would scrouge around wid deir tin cups and dip into de pan for de bean, pea, or turnip potliquor. Some funny scraps took place, wid de old mauma tryin' to separate de squallin', pushin', fightin' chillun.

BETTY POWERS: None of de infants suffers fo' de want of food 'cause dey am fed twice a day in de nursery. De infants gits plenty of food. 'Twas mostly milk wid co'nbread crumbled up in it, an' potliquor [liquid from cooked greens] wid co'nbread fixed de same way. Den 'twas little honey an' lots 'lasses [molasses] on bread. 'Twas good rations 'cause all de kids am fat lak little pigs. Ise can shut my eyes now, an' see all dem younguns a-sattin' 'round de big pans wid de wooden spoons, eatin' potliquor an' co'nbread.

Betty Powers at time of interview in Texas

NAP McQUEEN: Old Missus [slaveowner or slaveowner's wife] she good to dose chillen. She comes in herse'f every day to see dem and sometimes play with dem.

WILL RHYMES: He [slaveowner] played wid the li'l chillen, but was purty rough wid the ol'er ones [adults].

The Plantation Nursery

MANDY McCULLOUGH COSBY: I is now ninety-five years old an' what I remembers mos' is de way de chillun roll aroun' in de big nurse's room. Mist' McCullough he raised niggahs to sell. The little black chillen play aroun' until 'bout sundown, [then] dey is give dey supper. A long trough out in a cool place in the backyard is filled wif good, cold buttermilk an' cornbread crumbed in. Dey each is give a spoon an' dey eats dey fill. Den dey is ready fo' bed. Some of dem jes' fall ovah on de groun', asleep, and is picked up and put on dey pallet in de big chillen's room. Dey [There] was old woman called de nurse [who would] look after 'em. Dey git good care fo' de master expects dey will bring good money.

On some plantations, there were no provisions for a nursery:

AGNES JAMES: I never didn' work in no field or nothin' like dat no time. When I was a little small girl, I would stay dere [at] home en' play 'bout de yard en' nurse [take care of] my mammy's baby while she was workin' in de field.

Mary Kincheon Edwards, age 127 (born July 8, 1810) at time of interview

MARY KINCHEON EDWARDS: De women brung oil cloths to de fields so dey make shady place for de chillen to sleep, but dem what big 'nough has to pick [crops in the fields].

JOSIE BROWN: When us little, dey hab to keep us in de house 'cause de bald eagle pick up chillen jus' like de hawk pick up chicken. Dey was lots of catamoun' [mountain cats in Texas = cougars] and bears and deer in de woods. Us never 'lowed play 'lone in de woods.

MATTIE GILMORE: When dey's hoein' cotton or corn, everybody has to keep up with de driver, not hurry so fast, but workin' steady. Some de women what had suckin' babies left dem in de shade while dey worked. One time a big, bald eagle flew down by one dem babies and picked it up and flew away with it. De mama couldn't git it and we never heard of dat baby 'gain.

FOOD

HILLIARD YELLERDAY: Some owners gave their slaves the same kind of food served on their own tables and allowed the slaves the same privileges enjoyed by their own children. Other masters fed their slave children from troughs made very much like those from which the hogs of the plantation were fed.

MARY JANE KELLEY: Marse fed slaves in a trough in de yard.

PAULINE GRICE: De kind of feed weuns chilluns get? Well, it am milk an' mush mostest, wid some veg'ables an' fruit.

Pauline Grice, age 81 at time of interview

Food

PETER MITCHELL: We gits plenty cornbread and soup and peas. On Sunday, dey gives us jus' one biscuit apiece and we totes [carry] it 'round in de pocket half de day and shows it to de others [whose parents did not work in the Big House], and says, "See what we has for breakfast."

ANNA MILLER: We keeps full on what we gits, such as beans, co'nmeal, and 'lasses. We seldom gits meat. White flour — we don' know what dat taste like, jus' know what it looks like. We gits 'bout all de milk we wants 'cause dey puts it in de trough and we helps ourselves. Dere was a trough for de niggers and one for de hawgs.

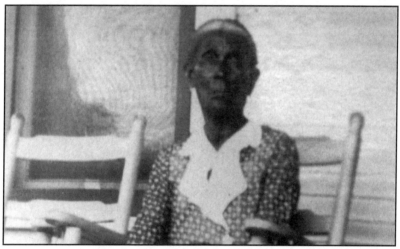

Adeline Cunningham, age 85 at time of interview

ADELINE CUNNINGHAM: Dey has a big trough jes' like de trough for de pigs. Dey has a big gourd and dey totes de gourd full of milk and dey breaks de bread in de milk. Den my mammy take a gourd and fills it and gives it to us chillun. How's we eat it? We had oyster shells for spoons. De [adult] slaves comes in from de fields and dey hands is all dirty, and dey is hungry. Dey dips dey dirty hands right in de trough and we can't eat none of it.

STEVE ROBERTSON: Allus kids am given de wooden spoon each. Dat's so's weuns won't cut de mouth w'en weuns eats. Well, weuns am lined up 'long de table. De table am 'bout 15 feet long, an' 'bout three feet wide. Den de nigger womans dat cares fo' de nursery kids, puts de wooden bowls — dey am 'bout two feet long — on de table. De bowls have skimmed milk wid all de clabbah dat am left f'om cookin' in de bowls. Den co'nbread am crumbled in it. If dere am no co'nbread left, den dey cooks co'n pone special fo' weuns. Dat am de reason dat weuns am fat lak de pigs.

MILLIE BARBER: Us never git butter or sweet milk or coffee. Dat was for de white folks. But in de summertime, I minds de flies off de table wid the peafowl feather brush and eat in de kitchen just what de white folks eat. Them was very good eatin's, I's here for to tell you. All de old slaves and them dat worked in de field got rations and de chillun were fed at de kitchen outhouse. What did they git? I 'members they [adults] got peas, hog meat, cornbread, 'lasses [molasses], and buttermilk on Sunday, then they got greens, turnips, 'taters [potatoes], shallots, collards, and beans through de week. They were kept fat on them kind of rations.

FRANK MENEFEE: All the chillun had a tin plate an' a tin cup with buttermilk in hit [it].

JENNIE BOWEN: Us house niggers et [ate] in de kitchen dat was separated f'om de main buildin' [from the slaveowner's house] by a walkway kivered [covered] at de top but not at de sides.

WILL ADAMS: The old heads got out early, but us young scraps slep' 'til eight or nine o'clock. Don't you think Massa Dave ain't comin' 'round to see we is fed. I 'members him like it was yest'day, comin' to the quarters with his stick and askin' us, "Had your breakfas'?" We'd say, "Yes, suh." Then he'd ask if we had 'nough or wanted any more. It look like he taken a pleasure in seein' us eat.

WILLIAM HENRY DAVIS: Dey want de chillun to hurry en' grow. Dat de reason dey give 'em good attention at de house.

ORELIA ALEXIE FRANKS: Lots of time we eat couscous. Dat make out of meal and water. You bile [boil] de water and salt it, den put in de cornmeal and stir it and bile it. Den you puts milk or clabber or syrup on it and eat it.

Food

REBECCA JANE GRANT: All of us chillun [who were] too little to work used to have to stay at de "Street" [the road through the slave quarters]. Dey'd have some old folks to look after us — some old man or some old woman. Dey'd clean off a place on de ground near de washpot where dey cooked de peas, clean it off real clean, den pile de peas out dere on de ground for us to eat. We'd pick 'um up in our hands and begin to eat. Sometimes dey'd cook hoe cakes in a fire of coals. Dey'd mix a little water with de meal and make a stiff dough that could be patted into shape with de hands. De cakes would be put right into the fire, and would be washed off clean after they were raked out from de coals.

ALEX WOODS: Missus [the slaveowner or the slaveowner's wife] chewed our food for us when we wus small. De babies wus fed wid sugar tits [a sweet pacifier sometimes tied on a string around their necks] and the food Missus chewed. Deir suckled mothers suckled [breastfed] dem at dinner, an' den [the mothers] stayed in de field 'til night.

TOB DAVIS: Thar am a thing weuns use to do dat Ise lak [like] well. 'Twas cookin' 'taters [potatoes, usually sweet potatoes] in de hot embers in de fireplace. In de wintah time, weuns often puts 'taters in de embers, wait fo' dem to bake, den sat in f'ont of de fireplace an' eat dem. Sometimes Mammy sings songs w'en weuns am sattin' thar. Now w'en Ise thinks 'bout it, tears comes to dis old nigger's eyes. Mammy use to cook beans in de embers. She puts dem in a closed skillet, a big one 'cause it tooks lots of beans. Dem am de bestest eatin' youse can git.

CLOTHING

ALEX WOODS: We wove our clothes — children had only one piece, a long shirt. We went barefooted an' in our shirttails, we youngins did.

WILLIS EASTER: All us chillen weared lowel white duckin', homemake, jes' one garment. It was de long shirt. You couldn't tell gals from boys in de yard.

A.C. PRUITT: I's jes' de li'l chile den, runnin' 'round in my split shirttail. Dey make 'em on de loom, jes' in two pieces with a hole to put de head through and 'nother hole at de bottom to put de legs through. Den dey split 'em up de side, so's us could run and play without dem tyin' us 'round de knees and throw us down. Even at dat, dey sho' wasn't no good to do no tree climbin', less'n you pull dem 'mos' up over you head.

CHRIS FRANKLIN: Dey all wear de straight-cut slip. Dey give de li'l gals de slip dress [a dress made like a slip] and li'l panties. In wintertime, dey give de boys de li'l coat and pants and shoes, but no drawers or unnerwear.

AMY PERRY: Dey ain't know nutting 'bout drawers [underwear] nor nutting like dat.

BUD JONES: I weared split shirts 'til I was nearly growed. I wanted me a little pair of pants, but I'm tellin' the truth when I say I didn't wear nothin' — nothin' a-tall [at all], for the most part, 'cept that shirt. I went in the snow barefoot. When I was bigger, they got me brass stud shoes and a hat once a year, but no pants.

ZEK BROWN: Ise 'membahs de last dress Ise wore. 'Twas a linsey cloth lak homespun am, wid stripes. Dat am de last dress. Aftah dat, Ise put in pants.

ANDREW GOODMAN: In summer, we wore long shirts, split up the sides, made out of lowerings — that's same as cotton sacks was made out of. In winter, we had good jeans and knitted sweaters and knitted socks.

ANNA MILLER: Weuns makes all de cloth for to makes de clothes, but we don' git 'em. In de winter, we 'mos' freeze to death.

WILLIS WOODSON: I stays in de house [lived in the slaveowner's house], so I gits good clothes and shoes, too. Some dem niggers didn't have hardly no clothes, though.

ANNIE OSBORNE: Old Man Tom never give us no money and half

Clothing

'nough clothes. I had one dress the year 'round, two lengths of cloth sewed together.

JIM HENRY: De Brattons was always sheep raisers, and us had woolen blankets and woolen clothes in de winter. My mother was one of de seamstresses. She make clothes for de slaves.

PREELY COLEMAN: Massa Tom made us wear the shoes 'cause they's so many snags and stumps our feets gits sore. They was red russet shoes. I'll never forgit 'em. They was so stiff at first we could hardly stand 'em.

Preely Coleman, age 85

Wes Brady, age 88

WES BRADY: I never had shoes on 'til after surrender come. I run all over the place 'til I was a big chap in jes' a long shirt with a string tied 'round the bottom for a belt.

MARY SELLERS: We went barefooted all the time except when it was too cold. Then the master would get shoes and stockings for us.

GORDON BLUFORD: In the wintertime, I didn't have much clothes and no shoes.

NICEY PUGH: For Sunday, us had mingled calico dresses dat us wore tuh church when us went.

CARRIE DAVIS: We wore 'em [the same clothes] Sunday and Monday de same. Us shoes was made at a tanyard and dey was brogans as hard as rocks.

LILA NICHOLS: We ain't had half 'nuff [enough] ter eat most of de time, an' we ain't had no shoes 'til we wuz twenty-one. We had jist a few pieces of clothes an' dey wuz of de wust [worst] kind.

MARTIN RUFFIN: Each nigger had his task and the chillen gathered berries in the woods to make dyes for clothes. Us [children] wore only white lowell clothes, though. They was sho' thick and heavy.

WILLIAM MATHEWS: De clothes we wore was made out of dyed 'lows.' Dat de stuff dey makes sackin' out of. Summertime us go barefoot, but wintertime come, dey give you shoes with heels on 'em big as biscuits.

FRANK MENEFEE: Had long shirt dresses of orsenberg dyed with red mud an' cinnamon bark. In winter, dey doubled de orsenberg to be warmer. My daddy was a shoemaker. He made dem outer cowhides an' even lef' de hair on dem sometimes.

JENNY PROCTOR: On Sunday, dey make all de chillun change. What we wears 'til we gits our clothes washed wuz gunny sacks wid holes cut for our head and arms.

ANNE BROOME: De boys run 'round in their shirttails and de girls just a one-piece homespun slip on in de summertime. Us didn't know and didn't care nothin' 'bout a 'spectable 'pearance [meaning they didn't have underwear] in those days. Dat's de truth, us didn't.

PLAYTIME

HENRY LEWIS [2]: Eben de chilluns had ter wuk f'om de time dey big ernuff ter fotch [fetch] er pail ob water er a load ob cobs. Dey didn't play much 'cep w'en dey off in de woods ter git de eggs, er de calves, er sometimes ter go fishin'.

JOHN PRICE: Us chillen have lots of time to play and not much

Playtime

time to work. Us allus [always] ridin' old stick hosses and tie a rope to de stick and call it a martingale. Us make marbles out of clay and dry 'em and play with 'em.

CAMPBELL DAVIS: Mos' de time us chillen play, makin' frog holes in de sand and mud people and things.

HENRY LEWIS [1]: Dey 'low de li'l chillen lots of playtime and no hard task. Us play stick hoss and seven-up marble game with marbles us make and de "Well Game." De gal or boy sot in de chair and lean way back and 'tend [pretended] like dey in de well. Dey say dey so many feet down and say, "Who you want pull you out?" And de one you want pull you out, dey s'posed to kiss you.

Campbell Davis, age 85

SALLY BANKS CHAMBERS: Us jump de rope and play dolls wid dolls mek wid weeds tie' togedder.

SALLY MURPHY: Us played jump rope and swung in de grapevine swings mostly. Den us had rag dolls.

KATHERINE EPPS: Us useta play "Sail Away Rauley" a whole lot. Us would hol' han's an' go 'roun' in a ring, gittin' faster an' faster. Dem what fell down was outa de game.

VICTOR DUHON: I didn't play much with the black children. My time went waiting on my white folks.

ANNIE OSBORNE: I didn't know nothin' 'bout playin'. If I made too much fuss [noise], they put me under the bed.

ELLEN PAYNE: We told ghost stories among ourselves that we made up.

I WAS A SLAVE

JOHN N. DAVENPORT: Dey played anti-over by a crowd gitting on each side of de house and throwing a ball from one side to de other. Whoever got de ball would run around on de other side and hit somebody wid it; den he was out of de game.

DELLIE LEWIS: Us useta play "Puss in de Cawner", "Next Do' Neighbor" an' "Fox an' Geese." I kin gib you some of de songs we useta sing:

"Old sweet beans an' barley grows,
Old sweet beans an' barley grows,
You nor I nor nobody knows
Where old sweet beans an' barley grows.

Go choose yo' east
Go choose yo' wes',
Go choose de one dat you love best.
If she's not here to take her part,
Choose de nex' one to yo' heart."

Julius Nelson, age 77, NC

JULIUS NELSON: We little'uns 'ud play "Fox on de Wall", tag, "Mulberry Bush", "Drap Handerchief", "Stealin' Sticks", an' a whole heap of others dat I disremembers right now.

EVA MARTIN: Dey was seben li'l white chillen and seben li'l nigger chillen, and us all play togedder. De littles' ones all hab de same nurse. Ol' Missus nurse 'em all from her own breas'. When my mammy hab a kid, Missus hab one, too. My mammy she go to wuk de nex' day atter she hab de kid and Ol' Missus she nurse 'em bofe [both] so Mammy ain't loss no time outer de fiel'. Dem slavery days.

And, of course, the children misbehaved:

FRANK MENEFEE: Us used to play "Green Grow the Willow Tree", you swing my gal an' I swing yourn. Dey [their parents and others] used to sceer up [scare] us niggers 'bout "Raw Head" an' "Bloody Bones" gwine to ketch us dat was so sceer bad iffen us didn't mind 'em [were going to catch us, who were scared so badly, if we didn't obey the adults].

Playtime

SALLIE PAUL: Cose, when we was chillun, de grown people would be force to punish us some of de time. Yes, ma'm, I do know what would happen to me if I been get in devilment. I would get a whippin' right den en' dere. I recollects dey would whip us chillun wid tree switches 'round us legs. Den if dey would want to spare de punishment, dey would try to scare us out de mischief. Tell us "Bloody Bones" would jump out dat corner at us if we never do what dey say do.

WORK

Children under the age of 12 years:

WALTER RIMM: I'se put to wo'k wid tudder kids jus' soon's [as soon as] I'se able to be took f'om de nursery. Weuns pulls weeds ha'f de day, put to sleep, den woke up to pull mo' weeds.

JACOB BRANCH: Us chillen start to work soon's us could toddle. First us gather firewood. Iffen it freezin' or hot, us have to go to toughen us up. When us git li'l bigger, us tend de cattle and feed hosses and hawgs [hogs]. By time us good sprouts, us pickin' cotton and pullin' cane. Us ain't never idle. Sometime us git far out in de field and lay down in de corn row and nap. But, Lawdy, iffen dey cotch you, dey sho' wore you out [spanked you hard]! Sunday de onliest rest day and den de white folks 'low us play.

REUBEN FITZPATRICK: My marster wuz Mister Gholson from Bullock County. He had lots uv slaves. He wuz a rich man. I wuz jes' a boy ten years ol' an' he wuz a squire dat tried cases, so he rode all over de country to diff'unt places. I rode wid him to hol' his horse.

STEVE ROBERTSON: Allus kids am put to knockin' stalks wid sticks. Dat's cotton stalks w'en dey's all dried up in de fall. Well, den weuns goes 'long an' thins de co'n wid our hands 'stead wid de hoes lak dey does now. Weuns stripped foddeh by cuttin' de tops ob de co'n fo' to feed de stock, an' also weuns gathahs de eggs. De mistez brags on de one [child] dat brings in de mostest eggs. Dat kinda spurs weuns up little bit on de egg huntin'. [Chickens ran free in the yards and in the woods.]

LIZZIE WILLIAMS: All de little niggahs have to learn to work when dey little — get out'n pull weeds. Dey neber had no time to play.

CURETON MILLING: I was just a little shrimp durin' slavery time [and was required to] tote water and ride behin' in de buggy to hold Marster's hoss when he gits out.

JOHN CRAWFORD: Ma's name was Viney Rector and the old jedge [judge] brung her from Alabama. She milked all the cows two times a day and I had to turn out all de calves.

John Crawford, age 81

WILLIAM DAVIS: 'Bout de first I 'members real good am where we am in Virginny and Massa John runs de Washington College in Washington County. I 'member all de pupils eats at Massa's house and dat de first job I ever had. 'Scuse me for laughin', but I don't reckon I thunk of dat since de Lawd know when. Dat my first job. Dey has a string fasten to de wall on one side de room, with pea fowl tail feathers strung 'long it. It runs most de length de room, above de dinin' table, and 'round a pulley-like place in de ceilin' with one end de string hangin' down. When mealtime come, I am put where de string hang down and I pulls it easy like. De feathers swishes back and forth sideways, and keeps de flies from 'lightin' while folks am eatin'.

WILL DAILY: Soon as I wuz big enough, about four or five years ol', Ol' Miss she starts trainin' me fer a houseboy. I's a-doin' all sorts of chores by de time I wuz six years old. Den Ol' Marster he starts sendin' me out on de plantation to drive up de hosses. I sho' likes dat job 'cause ain't nothin' I loves any better den hosses. Den when I wuz bigger, he starts me to carryin' de breakfast to de field whar de grown niggers had been out workin' since way 'fore day [before dawn].

HENRY LEWIS [1]: When I six or seven year old, dey 'cides I's big 'nough to start ridin' hosses. Dey have de big cattle ranch [in Texas] and I ride all over dis territory. I's too li'l to git on de hoss and dey lift me up. Dey have de real saddle for me, too. I couldn't git up, but I sho' could stay up when I git dere. I's jis' like a hossfly.

CAMPBELL ARMSTRONG: I wasn't doin' nothin' but totin' water. I toted water for a whole year when I was a boy about eight years old. I was the water boy for the field hands. Later I worked out in the fields myself. They would make me sit on my mammy's row to help keep her up [to help her to meet her quota of work].

TOM WILCOX: I wuz nine when de war commence. Durin' de war, I wuz workin' in de fiel' 'long wid de fifty or sixty other slaves.

MARY MORIAH ANNE SUSANNA JAMES: When I was ten years old, I was put to work on the farm with other children, picking weeds, stone up [picking up and piling stones] and [removing] tobacco worms and to do other work.

JACOB BRANCH: When I 'bout ten, dey sets me ginnin' cotton. Old Massa he done make de cotton with de hand crank. It built on a bench like. I gin de cotton by turnin' dat crank. When I gits a lapful, I puts it in de tow sack and dey take it to Miss Susan to make de twine with it. I warm and damp' de cotton 'fore de fireplace 'fore I start ginnin' it.

MARTIN RUFFIN: I wasn't big enough to tote water to the field when war started, but I driv [driv, pronounced like give, = drove] up the cows and calves and helped 'tend Massa's chillen. I was only eleven year old when the niggers was freed.

JOHN FINNELY: De wo'k am divided 'twix de cullud fo'ks. Allus have de certain duties to do. I's am a field hand. Befo' I's ol' 'nough fo' to do dat, deys have me he'p wid de chores an' run errands. I's 'bout 12 yeahs ol' w'en I's put to plowin' an' hoein' an' sich.

Children aged 12 years and older:

NELLIE LOYD: I belonged to Mr. George Buchanan. He was good to his slaves and never allowed any Negro under 12 years of age to work in the fields. I helped around the house until I was 12 years old.

SALLIE PAUL: You see, dey didn' work de chillun when dey was little bit of things en' stunt dem up. Chillun grow to be about 12 or 13 years old 'fore dey work dem in dat day en' time.

JOHN SNEED: Massa never 'low no whippin' of de chillen. He make dem pick rocks up and make fences out dem, but he didn't 'low no chillen work in de field 'til dey 'bout fourteen.

JORDON SMITH: Missus didn't 'low her niggers to work 'til they's 12. The first work I done was hoeing. Us worked long as we could see a stalk of cotton or hill of corn. It was Hell 'mong the yearlin's if you crost him or Missus, either. It was double trouble and a cowhidin' [whipping with a rawhide whip] whatever you do. She had a place in the kitchen where she tied their hands up to the wall and cowhided them and sometimes cut they back 'most [almost] to pieces.

ADELINE HALL JOHNSON: I never have to do no field work, just stayed 'round de house and wait on de mistress and de chillun. In de evenin', I fill them boxes wid chips and fat splinters [to use as kindling for the fireplace]. When mornin' come, I go in dere and make a fire for my young mistresses to git up by. I help dress them and comb deir hair. Then I goes downstairs and put flowers on de breakfas' table and lay de Bible by Marse William's chair. Then I bring in de breakfas'. When everything was on de table, I ring de bell. White folks come down and I wait on de table. After de meal finish', Marse William read de Bible and pray. I clear de table and help wash de dishes. When dat finish, I cleans up de rooms. I warms up de girls' room, where they sleep, after supper.

RYER EMMANUEL: Dey had to be over 16 year old 'fore old Massa would allow dem to work 'cause he never want to see his niggers noways stunt up while dey was havin' de growin' pains. Den when dey was first grow up, dey would give some of dem a house job en' would send de others in de field to mind de cows en' de sheep en' bring dem up. Wouldn't make dem do no heavy work right to start wid. But, dem what was older, dey had to work in de field.

CINTO LEWIS: I fust went to de field when I was 'bout 15 years old, but they learn us to work when we was chaps [children], little chaps. Sometimes our mammas would have to help us out on our row so we don't get whupped.

RICHARD JONES: After I was seventeen, I did all kinds of hoeing and plowing and other farm work fer my marster. He said dat, by dis time, his little niggers' bones had done got hard enough fer dem to work. Fer my first task, I had one-fourth of an acre in 'taters [potatoes], 'bacca [tobacco], and watermelons de first year. Some of de boys had 'inders [pinders = peanuts?], cantloupes, and matises (tomatoes) in deir task of a one-fourth acre.

SIMON GALLMAN: I was about twelve years old when dey made me go to de field to work. Befo' dat and after dat, too, I worked around de barn and took care of de stock.

ISOM NORRIS: Ise can't forget de ol' tan yard [tanning yard where shoes and other leather items were made], for de fus' job I had wuz getting de Red Oak bark for to use on de hides w'en we shaked dem in de vats to git de hair off.

JESSIE PAULS: Me no 'member de time w'en [I don't remember the exact time], but old Mistez Rindy larn me to drive de carriage w'en Walter gits old 'nough to go to reg'lar school. She do dat so's me drive her to town aftah de mail an' what else she wants in town. Me gits it in de neck w'en [It's a big problem for me when] she don't want me to drive her an' Walter am in school 'cause den me have to wo'k in de field. Me strip de cane fo' to put in de syrup mill, gits kindlin' [sticks and small pieces of wood] fo' de fire fo' de syrup mill, an' kindlin' fo' de house fire, hoe an' pick cotton, or what else dey wants me to do.

ANNA MILLER: My work 'twas helpin' wid de chores and pick up de brush whar my pappy was a-clearin' de land. When I gits bigger, Ise plowed, hoed, and done all de goin' to de mill. De weavin' was de night work, after workin' all de day in de fiel'. Ise helps card, spins, and cuts de thread.

STEVE ROBERTSON: Dere am one wo'k dat am mostest 'portant to me. Dat's de wo'k dat my mammy does aftah she wo'ks all day in de field. W'en Ise wo'k fo' my mammy, Ise runs de spinnin' wheel. Ise turns it fo' her. Dat way, I's 'lowed to stays up wid de old fo'ks [adults] an' heahs dem talk 'bout dis an' dat.

Dere am one tudder thing dat Ise he'ps wid on de old place. Dat am de t'baccy makin'. Dey grows it, an' w'en it am right to gathah, de old fo'ks brings in de leaves. Deys have de boxes, all sizes. Weuns tooks de t'baccy leaf, lays it on de bottom ob de box, tooks sugah, 'lasses, anything sweet lak dat, an' spreads it over de leaf, den puts tudder leaf, an' so on 'til de box am full an' de lid am nailed on. W'en dey wants t'baccy, deys opens de box, an' dere am t'baccy dat am sho' 'nough t'baccy!

DOZIER WASHINGTON: Hadder do some sorta work in dem days, lak hoe corn en' re-plant en' so on lak dat, but ne'er didn't do no man work. Wuz jes' uh half-hand [meaning a child did half the amount of work that an adult did], dat is 'bout so.

Work

LUCY GALLMAN: I was a girl in slavery, worked in the fields from the time I could work at all, and was whipped if I didn't work. I worked hard.

GUS FEASTER: De furs' work dat I done was drapping peas [dropping peas as a part of planting]. Albert [his brother] was plowhand when I come into de world. Harriet [his sister] was up big enough to plant corn and peas, too. Billy [his brother] looked atter de stock and de feeding of all de animals on de farm.

JAKE COMPTON: When I wuz jes' a boy, I used to help to cut de oats with a cradle an' tie dem with my hands.

James Cape at time of interview, approximately 100 years old

JAMES CAPE: When I's old 'nough to set on de hoss, dey larned me to ride, tendin' hosses [in Texas]. 'Cause I's good hoss rider, dey uses me all de time gwine after hosses.

PREELY COLEMAN: I grows big 'nough to hoe and den to plow. We has to be ready for the field by daylight. The conk was blowed and Massa call out, "All hands ready for the field." At 11:30, he blows the conk, what am the mussel shell, you knows, 'gain and we eats dinner [now called lunch], and at 12:30, we has to be back at work.

JOHN WALTON: I done field work up dere and even us kids had to pick 150 pounds cotton a day, or git de whoppin'. Us sho' was tired.

ANNIE OSBORNE: My white folks didn't teach us nothin' 'cept how they could put the whip on us. I had to put on a knittin' of stockin's [had to knit stockings, meaning long socks] in the mornin' and if I didn't git it out [didn't finish the task] by night, Missy put the lash on me.

THOMAS COLE: When I got older, he started me workin' by totin' wood and sech odd jobs, and feedin' de hawgs. Us chillen had to pick cotton every fall. De big baskets weigh about seventy-five to a hundred pounds, but us chillen put our pickin's in some growed slave's basket. De growed slaves was jes' like a mule. He work for grub [food] and clothes and some of dem didn't have as easier a time as a mule, for mules was fed good and slaves was sometimes half-starved.

WILLIS EASTER: All de lint was picked by hand on our place. It a slow job to git dat lint out de cotton. I's gone to sleep many a night, settin' by de fire, pickin' lint. In bad weather, us sot by de fire and pick lint and patch harness and shoes, or whittle out something, dishes and bowls and troughs and traps and spoons.

JENNIE FITTS: Ise wid Missy Annie alls de time and 'tend to her. Ise wid her night and day. Ise sleeps at de foot ob her bed. Ise keeps de flies off her wid de fan, gets her drink and sich, goes places fo' to get things fo' her. When she am ready to go to sleep eber [every] night, Ise rub her feet. Ise sho' 'tend to Missy.

MATTIE GILMORE: I worked in the fields 'til [sister] Rachel was sold, den tooken her place, doin' kitchen work and fannin' flies off de table with a great long limb. I liked dat. I got plenty to eat and not so hot [as working in the fields].

BUD JONES: It was my main most job to bring in the wood. I brung in the big, back logs when I was jus' a little boy. We kept big, blazin', roarin' fires. Then I had to feed the bloodhounds. Old Master had eight of 'em. They was smart dogs. If a nigger taken to the woods, Master put the dogs on him and that nigger'd have to take to a tree. Master said his dogs was trained not to tear a nigger up when they cotch him. They jus' grab a-holt of the nigger's clothes and helt him

Work

'til Master put a rope 'round him and brung him to the bull pen.

BETTY POWERS: Ise old 'nough to fan flies off de white fo'ks an' off de tables w'en dey eats w'en surrendah comes. Ise 'membahs 'cause 'tis de fust whuppin's Ise gits. 'Twas once w'en Ise failed to see some flies on de table an' de Marster had comp'ny fo' dinnah. De daughter tooks me upstairs an' use de whup [whip] on me. Mary am her name.

William Moore, age 82

WILLIAM MOORE: Marse Tom had a fine, big house painted white and a big prairie field [in Texas in] front his house and two, three farms and orchards. He had five hundred head of sheep. I spent mos' my time bein' a shepherd boy. I starts out when I'm li'l and larns right fast to keep good count of the sheeps.

JOHN MAJORS: My pappy wuz named Lee Majors after his master. Dis master lived on a plantation an' wuz an old bachelor. My pappy wuz his body servant. From de time I wuz nine years old w'en de Civil War broke out, I helped my pappy in de house. Dey called me de house boy. I run errands like going to de post office for de mail an' waitin' on de master w'en my pappy wuz busy wid other things.

GEORGE THOMPSON: As there were no oil lamps or candles, another black boy and myself were stationed at the dining table to hold grease lamps for the white folks to see to eat. We would use brushes to shoo away the flies.

PERRY MADDEN: My brother was big enough to mind gaps. They had good fences around the field. They didn't have gates like they do now. They had gaps. The fence would zigzag, and the rails could be lifted down at one section, and that would leave a gap. If you left a gap, the stock [cattle] would go into the field. When there was a gap, my brother would stay in it and keep the stock from passing. It took time to lay the rails down and more time to place them back up again. They wouldn't do it. They would leave them down 'til they come back during the work hours. A boy that was too small to do anything else was put to mind them. My brother used to do that and I [who was too young for this type of work] would keep him company.

ELLEN BUTLER: They have 'bout 200 head of niggers. When I gets big enough, they start me to totin' water to the field. I gits the water out the spring and totes it in gourds. They cut the gourds so that a strip was left 'round and 'cross the top and that' the handle. They was about a foot 'cross and a foot deep. Us used to have one good gourd us kep' lard in and li'l gourds to drink out of.

HENRY KIRK MILLER: As fast as us children got big enough to hire out, she [the mistress] leased us to anybody who would pay for our hire. I was put out with another widow woman who lived about 20 miles. She worked me on her cotton plantation. Old Mistress sold one of my sisters and took cotton for pay.

CAROLINE FARROW: My mistress had me to work in de house, kind of a housegirl, and she made me keep clean and put large earrings in my ears so I would look good.

BEN CHAMBERS: I driv [driv is pronounced like give] de kerrige to carry de white folks to chu'ch on Sunday. I hafter ketch ol' Tom and Bill, dey was de two kerrige hosses, and curry 'em and bresh 'em and keep de harness all oil' up, and hitch 'em up and drive to chu'ch. I keep dat buggy all clean up and lookin' nice. Dat was one of de bestes' tasks on de plantation and some of dem other niggers was sorter jealous of me.

Work

MARGARET HUGHES: I was too young to do much work, so the missus mostly keep me in de house to nurse [to take care of] de chillun. When de chillun go to school, she make me go 'long wid them for to look after them and tote their books. I stayed wid them all day [probably remaining outside the school] and brought their books home in de evening.

CHARLIE DAVIS: When I was a boy, I mind de crows out de field. Oh, crows was terrible 'bout pickin up people's corn in times back dere.

ANNIE ROW: Cloth for de clothes was made by de spinners and weavers and that what they larned [learned = taught] me to do. My first work was teasin' de wool. I bets you don't know what teasin' de wool am. It am pickin' de burrs and trash and sich out of de wool for to git it ready for de cardin'.

MARY REYNOLDS: I 'member I helt a hoe handle mighty onsteady when they put a old women to larn me and some other chillun to scrape the fields. That old woman would be in a frantic. She'd show me and then turn 'bout to show some other li'l nigger, and I'd have the young corn cut clean as the grass. She say, "For the love of Gawd, you better larn it right or Solomon will beat the breath out you body." Old Man Solomon was the nigger driver.

ADELINE MARSHALL: Cap'n [Captain] he a bad man, and he drivers hard, too, all de time whippin' and stroppin' de niggers to make dem work harder. Didn't make no difference to Cap'n how little you is, you goes out to de field 'mos' soon's [almost as soon as] you can walk. De drivers don't use de bullwhip on de little niggers [children], but dey plays [used] de switch on us what sting de hide plenty.

FRANK ADAMSON: What I do? Hoed cotton, pick cotton, tend to calves, and slop de pigs under de 'vision of de overseer. Who he wuz? First one name Mr. Cary, he a good man. Another one, Mr. Tim Gladden, burn you up whenever he just take a notion to pop his whip. Us boys run 'round in our shirttails. He lak to see if he could lift de shirttail widout techin' [touching] de skin. Just as often as not, though, he tech de skin. Little boy holler and Marster Tim laugh.

THE SLAVE CHILDREN AND THE SLAVEOWNER'S CHILDREN

Usually, slave children played only with each other. On many plantations, however, young slaves were allowed to play with the slaveowner's children. PLEASE REMEMBER that some slaveowners absolutely forbade them from associating with the white children at any time or from coming anywhere near the Big House.

JOHN COLLINS: My Marster had one son, Wyatt, and two daughters, Nannie and Elizabeth. They was all right, so far as I 'member, but being a field hand's child, off from de Big House, I never got to play wid them any.

LAURA THOMPSON: As children, we all played together, black and white. We didn't know nothing 'bout prejudice down in Kentucky when I was a child. When it came time for us to go to bed, my father would take all of the white children up to the master's house. White and colored children played together, but colored knowed their place.

ROSANNA FRAZIER: All us little chillen, black and white, play togedder and Marse Frasier he raise us. Marse Frasier he treat us nice and de other white folks calls us "free niggers" and wouldn't 'low us on deir places. Dey 'fraid deir niggers git dissatisfy with dey own treatment. Sho's you born [As sure as you're born = You can be absolutely certain], iffen one of us git 'round dem plantations, dey jus' cut us to pieces with de whip.

NELSON DORSEY: I remember one Christmas Day when I was little, my mother was very sick. The mistress came to our shack [and] took me up to the Big House because my mother was too sick to take care of me. My mistress had a little girl that was just three weeks older than I was, and she raised us together.

MINTIE MARIA MILLER: After we come to Texas, we live on a big place. It was somewhere 'round Lynchburg. Dr. Massie own it. He had two girls an' I use' to sleep on de foot of deir bed.

The Slave Children and the Slaveowner's Children

ROSIE McGILLERY: Ise played with the little white children 'cause my brothers was sold to another man before I got old enough to play with them. Ise always with the white children. We play "Wolf Over the River" and ring games where both old and young would take part. We would ring up [make a ring of people] and drop a rag behind someone, and that one [would try to] catch [the] one that dropped the handkerchief. If he didn't catch him, he would go in the middle of the ring. He couldn't get out unless he steals the rag from someone.

JOSIE BROWN: I didn' do nothin' 'cep' eat and sleep and foller ole mistus 'round. She give me good clothes 'cause my mudder was de weaver. De clothes jus' cut out straight down and dyed with all kin's of bark. I hab to keep de head comb and grease with lard. De lil' white chillun play with me, but not de udder nigger chilluns much. Us pull de long, leaf grass and plait it. Us make rag doll and playhouse and grapevine swing.

JOHN SNEED: Dere a big gang of white and cullud chillen on de plantation, but Dr. Sneed didn't have no chillen of he own. De neighbor white chillen come over dere and played. Us rip and play and fight and kick up us heels and go on.

THOMAS GOODWATER: Boys in dose days could fight, but couldn' throw anyone on the groun'. We had to stan' up an' eider [either] beat or git beat.

GABRIEL GILBERT: De li'l white folks and nigger chillen uster jis' play 'roun' like brudder and sister. Us all eat at de white table. Sometime' us boys hab fights. Us fight de white boys and niggers jis' de same. But dey's a big diff'rence 'tween de whites and de cullud folks now.

ANDREW GOODMAN: My missus was just as good as Marse Bob. I played 'round with little Miss Sallie and little Mr. Bob. I ate with them and slept with them. I used to sweep off the steps and do things. She'd brag on me and many is the time I'd git to noddin' and go to sleep, and she'd pick me up and put me in bed with her chillun.

ELVIRA BOLES: White folks' chillen had candy. We didn't git any bought candy, but dey let us play wid the white chillen [during Christmas]. They [There] was three or four. We'd play smut. The white folks'd give us cards and whoev'va beat, he git to smut yuh. Take de smut [burned black residue] from fiahplace [fireplace] and rub on yo' face.

CATO CARTER: Back in Alabama, Missie Adeline Carter took me when I was past my creepin' [crawling] days to live in the Big House with the white folks. I had a room built on the Big House where I stayed. They was allus good to me 'cause I's one of their blood. They never hit me a lick or slapped me once, and told me they'd never sell me away from them. They was the bes' quality white folks and lived in a big, two-story house with a big hall what run all the way through the house. They wasn't rough as some white folks on their niggers.

LU LEE: We played with the white chillen. I'd hear Master Davy call and say,"You got your school books out there?" and his chillen say, "Yes," and then he tells them, "Bring them books in the house and then you can go back and play." You see, they didn't want us nigger chillen to larn readin' or writin' 'cause then we'd know what's gwine on.

CHILDHOOD REMEMBRANCES

HENRY LEWIS [1]: Old Massa he a big, stocky Irishman with sandy hair and he ain't had no beard or mustache. When he grow old, he have de gout and he put de long mattress out on de gallery [long porch] and lay down on it. He say, "Come here, my li'l niggers," and den he make us rub he foots so he kin git to sleep.

BUD JONES: I didn't have no chilluns to play with. I jes' sat 'round studyin' [observing and thinking]. Old Master come in at night and say, "Bud, come here and cut me a step or two." He liked to see me dance. I had to dance for all the company. I did the "Ground Shuffle" and the "Pigeon Wing" and the "Back Step". I can still do them.

MARY REYNOLDS: I was born same time as Miss Sara Kilpatrick. Dr. Kilpatrick's first wife and my maw come to their time right together. Miss Sara's maw died and they brung Miss Sara to suck with me. It's a thing we ain't never forgot. We sucked 'til we was a fair size and played together, which wasn't no common thing. None the other li'l niggers played with the white chillun. But Miss Sara loved me so good.

Childhood Remembrances

I was just about big enough to start playing with a broom to go about sweepin' up and not even half doing it when Dr. Kilpatrick sold me. There was a old white man in Trinity whose wife died and he didn't have chick nor chile nor slave nor nothing. Marster sold me cheap 'cause he didn't want Miss Sara to play with no nigger youngun. That old man bought me a big doll and he went off and left me all day long with the door open. I just set on the floor and played with that doll. I used to cry. He would come home and give me something to eat and then go to bed. I slept on the foot of the bed with him. I was scared all the time in the dark. He never did close the door.

GUS FEASTER: Lots of times, Newt and Anderson [slaveowner's sons] would tell me and John [his older brother] to come and git under de steps while Ol' Marse was eating his supper. When he git up from de table, us li'l niggers would allus hear de sliding o' his chair kaise he was sech a big fat man. Den he go into de missus' room to set by de fire. Dar he would warm his feets and have his Julip [alcoholic drink]. Quick as lightning, me and John scamper from under de steps and break fer de big cape jasmine bushes 'long de front walk. Dar we hide 'til Anderson and Newt come out a-fetching ham biscuit in dey hands fer us. It would be so full of gravy dat sometime de gravy would take and run plumb [completely] down to de end o' my elbow and drap [drop] off 'fo' [before] I could git it licked off'n my wrists. Dem was de best rations dat a nigger ever had. When dey had honey on de white folks' table, de boys never did fail to fetch a honey biscuit wid dem. Dat was so good dat I jest take one measley li'l bite of honey and melted butter on my way to de quarter [the slave cabins]. I would jest taste a leetle [little]. When I git to Mammy, den me and Mammy set off to ourselfs and taste it 'til it done all gone.

ZENO JOHN: Sometime us chillen see 'em tekkin' a nigger off to whip him. Us try to foller and see what dey gwine do to him, but dey allus [always] mek us go back. Dey neber 'low us to see 'em whip him, but us could hear him holler.

WARREN McKINNEY: My ma was a slave in the field. I was eleven years old when freedom was declared. When I was little, Mr. Strauter whipped my ma. It hurt me bad as it did her. I hated him. She was crying. I chunked him with rocks. He run after me, but he didn't catch me.

GUS FEASTER: While de Yankees had everything closed up down in Charleston, it was hard to git anything in dis country into de sto's [stores]. Us allus traded at de post (Goshen Hill Trading Post). If I recollects correctly, it was during dis period dat Marse Tom let my mammy go up to de post to fetch back her a bonnet. [This slaveowner was extraordinarily lenient since most slaves rarely were allowed off the plantation. When they were permitted to go, they usually went to other plantations to visit or to run errands, not to town to make personal purchases. — Donna]

Up dar, dey took cotton and corn and anything like dat in trade dat dey could sell to de folks dat was working on de railroad bed (Seaboard Airline) dat was gwine through dat country. So, Mammy took a lot of cotton wid her to de post. I's gwine 'long wid her and so I had to wear some pants to go to de post as dat was big doings for a li'l darky boy to git to go to de trading center. So Aunt Abbie fotched me a pair of new pants dat was dat stiff dat dey made me feel like I was all closed up in a jacket, atter being used to only a shirttail.

Well, it wasn't fur and us arriv' dar early in de day. I seed so many things dat I never had seed befo', not in all my born days. Red sticks o' candy was a-laying right dar 'fo' [before] my eyes, jes' like de folks from de Big House brung us at Christmas. It was not near Christmas den kaise it was jest cotton-picking time and I wondered how-come [why] dey was having candy in de store fer, no-how [anyway].

"Marse, please sir, give me five cent worth peppermint candy." Den when he hand her de bag, she break off li'l piece and hand it to me, and [glare] her eyes at me and say in a low voice, "Don' you dare git none dat red on yo' clean shirt, if you wants to git home widout gitting wo' plumb smack out [getting worn completely out = getting spanked hard and long]."

Den she talk about de bonnets. Finally she git one fer ten dollars worth o' cotton. Money wasn't nothing in dem times. By dis time, us had done started on our return home and I was starting to feel more like I allus felt.

"Nigger, what dat you is done gone and got on dat clean shirt? Didn't you hear me tell you not to git dat new shirt all red? Look dar, a-streaming down off'n your chin, dat dar red. How is I gwine to ever teach you anything when you act jest like a nigger from some pore [poor] white trash's pore land? When we gits to dat branch [stream of water], now I's got to stop and wash dat dirty black mouth. Den I can't git dat red candy off'n dat shirt. What Ol' Lady Abbie gwine to say to ye when she see you done gone and act like you ain't never seed no quality befo'? Atter I has done tole you all de way from home how you must act at de post, den you goes and does like you is. Ain't never gwine to carry you nowhars 'gin long as I lives."

ALLEN SIMS

I 'members lots 'bout slavery times 'cause I was right dar. I don't 'member much 'bout de war 'cause I was too little to know what war was. De most I seed was when de Yankees come through and burnt up de Big House, de barns, de ginhouse, and took all Old Marster's hosses and mules, and kilt de milk-cows for beef. They didn't leave us nothing to eat, and us lak to starve to death.

Our folks, de Simses, dey come f'om Virginny. My pappy and mammy was borned dere. Dey names was Allen Sims and Kitty Sims. My old marster was Marse Jimmie Sims, and my old mistis was Miss Creasie. Some of Pappy and Mammy's chillun was borned in Virginny, and some of 'em in Alabama. I was de baby chile, and I was borned right on dis very place whar us is now [in Lee County, Alabama]. Dey had a whole passel of chillun. Dere was Chaney, Becky, Judy, Sam, Phoebe, King, Alex, Jordan, and Allen — dat's me.

Us lived in a log house in de quarter, wid a board roof and a big rock fireplace wid a stick and dirt chimley. We had plenty wood, and could build jes' as big a fire as we need if de weather was cold. Mammy she cook ashcake in de fireplace. It was de bes' bread I ever eat, better'n any dis store-bought bread. You ain't never eat no ashcake? Umph, Missy, you don't know what good bread is lak!

Old Marster was good to his niggers and all of 'em, big and little, had plenty to eat, and it wa'n't trash, neither. Us had ashcake, hoecake, ponebread, meat and gravy, peas, greens, roast-neers [roasting ears = corn on the cob], potliquor [liquid from cooked greens], sweet 'taters, I'ish 'taters, and goobers [peanuts]. I 'spec' [suspect] Old Marster's niggers live better dan lots of white folks lives now.

Aunt Mandy, what was too old to work, looked atter all de little nigger chilluns whilst dey mammys was working. She whip us wid a bresh [slender switches from trees with a few of the leaves still attached] if we didn't mind [obey] her. But she fuss more dan she whip and it didn't hurt much, but us cry lak she killing us.

When us got sick, Old Mistis looked atter us herself, and she gin [prepared] us oil and turpentine and lobelia. If dat didn't cure us, she sont for de doctor — de same doctor dat come to see her own fambly. Sometime a old nigger die, and Old Marster and Old Mistis dey cry jes' lak us did. Dey put 'em in a coffin and bury 'em in de graveyard wid de white preacher dar, and nobody didn't work none dat day atter us come back f'om de graveyard. [Many slaveowners did not allow funerals. At slave burials, there was seldom a preacher, much less a white one.]

Our beds was bunks in de corner of de room, nailed to de wall and jes' one post out in de flo'. De little chilluns slep' crosswise de big bed and it was plum' full [completely full of children] in cold weather.

Our clothes was orsenburg (Osnaburg), spun and weave right at home. It sho' did last a long time. De little niggers jes' wore a long shirt 'tel [until] dey got big 'nough to work in de field. Us had red shoes made at de tanyard to wear in wintertime, but us foots was tough and us went barefooted 'most all de winter, too. Us played games, too, ginerly [generally] jumping de rope and base.

De grown niggers had good times Sadday nights, wid dances, suppers, and wras'lin'. De cornshuckings was de biggest time dey had 'cause de neighbors come and dey laughed and hollered nearly all night. [Slaveowners who lived near each other would have all of their slaves go to one owner's plantation and then to another's. With all of the slaves from two or more plantations working on one plantation's crop, the shucking of corn would be faster. There usually was a festive atmosphere during which the slaves ate and drank as they worked. They sometimes competed to find a red ear of corn in order to win a kiss, or to shuck the most corn in the least time in order to win extra brandy or some other token.]

Old Marster and Old Mistis lived in a big two-story white house. Dey had ten chillun, five boys and five gals, and dey all growed up and married off. De old carriage driver was name' Clark and he sho' was proud. De overseer was Tetter Roberson and he was mean. He beat niggers a lot, and, by-me-by, Old Marster turned him off [fired him]. He used to blow de horn way befo' day to git de niggers up and he work 'em 'tel smack [completely] dark.

Atter de Yankees burned up every'ting 'cept de cabins, us jes' stayed right dar wid Old Marster when us freed. Old Marster built a new house for him and Old Mistis, but it wa'n't much better dan our cabin. Dey lived dere 'tel dey died.

When I growed up, I married Laura Frazier. Us had a big wedding and a preacher and didn't jump over no broom lak some niggers did. Us had jes' two chillun dat lived to be grown. Dey is Filmore and Mary Lou, and us ain't got no gran'chillun.

When I got grown, I j'ined de Baptist Church at Rough Neck 'cause I felt I had done enough wrong. I been a deacon forty year.

EDA RAINS

Eda Rains in Texas at time of interview

I don't 'member my first marster 'cause my mammy and Jim and John, who was my brothers, and me was sold [to a Mr. Carter] when I was seven and brought to Douglass, in Texas, to hire out [to be rented out to work for others]. Befor' we lef' Little Rock, whar I was born, we was vaccinated for smallpox. We came through in a wagon to Texas and camped out at night and we slep' on the groun'.

When I's hired out to the Tomlins at Douglass, I sho' got lonesome for I's jus' a little girl, you know, and wanted to see my mother. They put me to work pa'chin' [parching corn to be used as a substitute for] coffee and my arm was still sore. I'd pa'ch and cry, and pa'ch and cry. Finally Missus Tomlin say, "You can quit now." She looked at my arm and then put me to tendin' chillen. I was fannin' the baby with a turkey wing fan and I fell to sleep. When the missus saw me, she snatched the fan and struck me in the face with it. This scar on my forehead is from that quill stuck in my head.

I slep' on a pallet [quilts or other bedding on the floor] in the missus' room and she bought me some clothes. She had nine chillen, two boys and seven girls. But after awhile, she sol' me to Marster Roack, and he bought my mother and my brothers, so we was togedder again. We had our own cabin and two beds. Every day at four, they called us to the Big House and give us milk and mush. The white chillen had to eat it, too. It was one of Marster's ideas and he said he's raised that-a-way [that way].

Now, I mus' tell you all 'bout Christmas. Our bigges' time was at Christmas. Marster'd give us maybe fo' bits [four bits equals fifty cents, probably the total for the whole group of children] to spend as we wanted and maybe we'd buy a string of beads or some sech notion. On Christmas Eve, we played games, "Young Gal Loves Candy," or "Hide and Whoop." Didn' know nothin' 'bout Santa Claus, never was larned that. But we allus knowed what we'd git on Christmas mornin'. Old Marster allus call us togedder and give us new clothes — shoes, too. He allus wen' to town on the Eve and brung back our things in a cotton sack. That ol' sack'd be crammed full of things and we knowed it was clothes and shoes 'cause Marster didn' 'lieve in no foolishness. We got one pair shoes a year, at Christmas. Most times they was red and I'd allus [always] paint mine black. I's one nigger didn' like red. I'd skim grease off dishwater, mix it with soot from the chimney, and paint my shoes. In winter, we wore woolen clothes and got 'em at Christmas, too.

We was woke up in the mornin' by blowing of the conk. It was a big shell. It called us to dinner and if anything happened special, the conk allus blew.

I seed runaway slaves and Marster kep' any he caught in a room. He chained 'em 'til he cou' [could] reach their marsters.

We didn' get larned to read and write, but they took care of us iffen we was sick. We made medicine outta black willow and outta black snake root and boneset. It broke fevers on us, but, Lawsy, it was a dose.

After freedom, they tol' us we could go or stay. I stayed awhile. I married Clainborn [Clairborn?] Rains and lived at Jacksonville. We had ten chillen. The Lawd's been right good to me, even if I'm blind. Nearly all my ol' white folks and my chillen has gone to Judgment, but I know the Lawd won't leave me here too long 'fore I jines 'em.

ISAAC MARTIN

Dis ol' man jes' layin' 'roun'. Ain't nuttin' to him no mo'. I done wo' out. I jes' waitin' for de Good Marster to call po' ol' Isaac home to Glory.

When dey read de proclamation [declaring freedom] to my mammy and daddy, dey mek 'em give eb'rybody' age in de fam'ly. I was twelve year' ol' den.

I was bo'n up here in Montgomery County [Texas] 'bout t'ree mile from Willis upon de I&GN Railroad. I help to buil' dat I&GN Railroad.

Ol' Major Wood he my daddy' marster and, course, he mine, too. He was well fixed [rich]. He had 'bout seb'nty or eighty wukkin' slaves and I dunno how many li'l niggers [slave children]. I didn' know nuttin' 'bout Ol' Missus, Mrs. Wood. I jis' 'member she a big fat woman. Dey didn' 'low no li'l nigger chillun up in de yard 'roun' de Big House 'cep'n' to clean up de yard, and dem what done dat, dey hatter be jis' like dat yard, clean as peckerwoods.

Ol' Marster he warn't mean. He nebber whip' 'em jis' so iffen anybody say [He never whipped them just because someone said that] de slave orter be whip. Dey hafter see him and tell him what dey done befo' he give de order to de overseer to whip. Iffen he don' t'ink dey orter be whip, he say don' whip 'em and dey don' git whip.

I had to mind [take care of] de cows and de sheep. I had a mule to ride 'roun' on. It was dis way: I hafter mind de cows. Ol' Marster he plant dif'rent fiel's in co'n, fifty or sixty or a hundred acres. When dey harvestin' de co'n, when dey get one fiel' done, dey tu'n de cows in so dey kin eat on de stalks and nubbins what lef' in dat fiel'. I got to ride 'roun' and see de cows don' bus' over [don't bust over = don't break through the fence] from one fiel' what dey done harves' into de other fiel' where dey wukkin' or what ain't been harves' yet. I jis' like dat, ridin' dat mule 'roun' de

53

fiel' and keepin' de cows in.

Den dere was five or six of us boys to keep de dogs out de sheep. You know, iffen de dogs git in de sheep, dey ap' to kill 'em.

Us go huntin' wid de dogs lots of time, and lots of time us ketch rabbits. Dey was six dogs. De rabbits we kotch was so much vittles [food] for us. I 'member one night us went out huntin' and ketch fo' or five rabbits. Us tek 'em home and clean and dress 'em, and put 'em in de pot to have big rabbit supper. I was puttin' some red pepper in de pot to season 'em, and den I rub my eyes wid my han' and git dat pepper in my eyes and it sho' burn. You know how red pepper burn when it git in your eyes. I nebber will forgit 'bout dat red pepper. De ol' folks uster show us how to fix de t'ings we ketch huntin', and cook 'em.

Ol' Marster sho' t'ought mo' of his li'l nigger chillen. He uster ride in de quarters 'cause he like to see 'em come runnin'. De

This enlargement of the photograph on page 18 shows that both are barefooted.

Isaac Martin

cook she was a ol' woman name' Forney, and she had to see atter feedin' de chillen. She had a way of callin' 'em up. She holler, "Tee, tee, t-e-e," and all us li'l niggers jis' come runnin'. Ol' Marster he ride up and say, "Forney, call up dem li'l pickaninnies," and Ol' Forney she lif' up her voice and holler, "Tee, t-e-e, t-e-e," and Ol' Marster jis' set up on de hoss and laugh and laugh a lot to see us come runnin' up. He like to count how many li'l niggers he did have. Dat was fun for us, too. I 'member dat jis' like yestiddy.

Nuttin' went hard wid me. Fur's I know 'bout slav'ry, dem was good times. [Mr. Martin was young during slavery and, therefore, not old enough to do hard labor.]

Dey had 'bout t'ree or fo' hundred of sheep. My father hafter kill a mutton eb'ry Friday for de house. Dey bring up de sheep and somebody hol' de head 'cross a block and my father cut de head off wid a hatchet. Sheeps is de pitifullest t'ings to kill. Dey jis' give up. And dey cries, too. But a goat, he don' give up, naw suh, he talk back to you to de las'.

I 'member one time dey gwine to give a school feas' and dey gwine kill a goat. Dey hang dat goat up to a tree by he hind legs so de blood dreen [drains] good. Dey cut he t'roat, dat's de way dey gwine kill 'im. Dat goat seem like he kep' on talkin' and sayin', "Please, God, don' kill me" to de las', but dat ain't done no good. Dat goat jis' beg to de las'.

My ol' marster he live in a big house. Oh, it was a palace. It had eight or nine rooms. It was buil' outer logs, and moss and clay was stuff' 'twixt [between] de logs. Dere was boards on de outside and it was all seal' nice on de inside. He lived in a mansion.

Dey was plenty rich. Ol' Marster he had a ol' waitin' man all dress up nice and clean. Now if you wanter talk to Ol' Marster, you hafter call for dat ol' waitin' man. He come and you tell him what you want and den he go and tell Ol' Marster. Den he say, "Bring him in" and den you go in and see de ol' marster and talk your business, but you had to be nice and hol' your hat under your arm.

Dey's big rich people. Sometime dey have parties what las' a week. Dey was havin' deir fun in deir way. Dey come in kerridges and hacks.

My father was de hostler and he hafter keep de hosses [horses] and see 'bout feedin' 'em. Dey had a sep'rate li'l house for de saddles. Ol' Marster he kep' good hosses. He warn't mean.

He had a great big pasture and lots of times people go camp in it. You see, it was dis-a-way: De Yankees dey got rushin' de American people, dat de Confed'rates. Dey kep' comin' furder and furder wes' 'til dey come to Texas and den dey can't go much furder. De Yankees kep' crowdin' 'em and dey kep' on comin'. When dey camp in Ol' Marster' pasture, he give 'em co'n. I see 'em dribe a whole wagon load of co'n and dump it on de groun' for dey hosses. De Yankees nebber come 'til de war close. Den dey come all through dat country. Dat was destruction, it seem to me like. Dey take what dey want.

When freedom come and de proclamation was read and de ol' marster tol' 'em dey was free and didn' have no ol'marster no mo', some of de slaves cried. He tell 'em, "I don't want none of you to leave. I'll give you $8.00 a mont'." All de ol' folks stay and help gadder dat crop. It sho' griebe [grieved] Ol' Marster and he didn' live long atter dey tek his slaves 'way from him. Well, it jis' kill' him, dat's all. I 'members de Yankees on dat day dey sot [were sent] to read de proclamation. Dey was gwine 'roun' in dey blue uniform and a big long sword hangin' at dey side. Dat was cur'osity to dem niggers.

When Ol' Marster want to go out, he call he li'l nigger serbent to go tell my father, what was de hostler, to saddle up de hoss and bring him 'roun'. Den Ol' Marster git on him. He had t'ree steps so he could jis' go up dem steps and den his foot be right at de stirrup. My daddy hol' de stirrup for him to put he other foot in it.

I was big 'nuff to run after him and ax [ask] him to gimme a dime. He laugh and sometime he gimme de dime. Sometime he pitch it to me and I run and grab it up and say, "T'ankee, Marster," and he laugh and laugh.

Ol' Mistus she had a reg'lar cook. Dat was my mudder's mudder. Eb'ryt'ing had to be jis' so, and eb'ryt'ing nice and clean.

Dey didn' do no reg'lar wuk on Sunday. Eb'ry Sunday, one of de uther wimmins hafter tek de place of de cook so she could git off. All of 'em what could would git off and go to de chu'ch for de preachin'. Dem what turn didn' come one Sunday would go anudder 'til dey all get 'roun' to go.

Marster had two er t'ree hundred head of cattle. My

Isaac Martin

gran'father, Guilford, had [was allowed to keep] a mule and hoss of he own. Uncle Hank was his brudder, and he had de sheep department to look atter. Sometime de niggers git a hoss or a sheep over, den de Marster buy 'im. Some of de niggers had a li'l patch [garden] 'roun' dey cabin' and dey raise veg'table. Ol' Marster he buy de veg'table sometime. [This slaveowner was a rarity. Such practices almost never occurred on plantations.]

I didn' know what freedom was. I didn' know wedder I needed it or not. Seem to me like it was better den dan now [during the Great Depression of the 1930's] 'cause I gotter look out for myself now.

Us uster be on de watch-out for Ol' Marster. De fus' one see him comin' lit out [ran very fast] and open de gate for him to ride froo [through] and Ol' Marster toss him a nickle.

When it was time to eat, de ol' cook holler out, "T-e-e, t-e-e, t-e-e-e" and all us li'l niggers come runnin'. She have a big tray and each of us have a wessel and a spoon. She fill' us wessel and us go eat and den us go back for mo'. Us git all us want. Dey give us supper befo' de han's come in from de fiel'. What wid playin' 'roun' all day and eatin' all us could hol' in de afternoon, 'twarn't long befor' us li'l niggers ready to go to sleep.

One t'ing, Ol' Marster didn' want his niggers to run about. Sometime dey want to go over to anudder plantation on Sunday. Den he give 'em a pass iffen he willin' for 'em to go. Dey had patterrollers to ride from plantation to see iffen dey was any strange niggers dere. [See page 7.]

When dey wanter marry, de man he repo't to Ol' Marster. He want his niggers to marry on his own plantation. He give 'em a nice li'l supper and a big dance. Dey had some sort of license but Ol' Marster tek care of dat. [No license was required.] He had two sons what had farms and slaves of deir own. Ol' Marster didn' care if his slaves marry on his sons' farms. If any of de slaves do mean, he mek 'em work on Sunday. He didn' b'leeb in beatin' 'em.

So many of 'em as could usually go to de white folks' chu'ch on Sunday and hear de white preacher. Dey sit off to deyse'fs in de back of de chu'ch. Dem what stay at home have a cullud preacher. Dey try to raise 'em up social.

Dey had a ol' woman to look after de babies when dey mammies was out in de fiel'. Dey have a time sot [set] for de mammies to come in and nuss de babies. De ol' woman she had helpers. Dey had a big house and cradle' for dem babies where de nuss [nurse = caretaker] tek care of 'em.

When anybody die, dey have a fun'rel. All de han's knock off work to 'tend de fun'rel. Dey bury de dead in a ho'made coffin.

I nebber pay no 'tention to talk 'bout ghos'es [ghosts]. I nebber b'leeb in 'em. But one time comin' from chu'ch, my uncle' wife say, "Ike, you eber see a ghos'? Want to see one?" and I tell her "I don't give a cent. Yes, I want to see one." She say, "I show you a man dress' all in white what ain't got no head, and you gwine feel a warm breeze." After awhile, down de hill by de graveyard, she say, "Dere he go." I look' but I neber see nuttin', but I feel de warm breeze.

I uster go to see a gal [after Emancipation] and I uster hafter pass right by a ol' graveyard. It was all wall' up wid brick. But one place dey had steps up over de wall so when dey hafter bury a body, two men kin walk up dem steps side by side, and dat de way dey tek de corpse over. Well, when I git to dem steps, I hear sump'n'. Den I step and I ain't hear nuttin'. When I start walkin' ag'in, I hear de noise ag'in. I look 'roun' and den I see sump'n' white come up right dere where de steps go over de wall. I had a stick in my han' and nex' time it come up, I mek a rush at it and hit it. It was jis' a great big ol' billy goat what got inside de wall and was tryin' to git out. He get out jis' when I hit him and he lit out froo de woods. Dat's de only ghos' I eber see and I's glad dat warn't no ghos'.

Ol' Marster he had twenty head of cows. Dey give plenty milk. Dey uster git a cedar tub, big as dat dere one, full of milk. De milkers dey pack it [carry it] on dey head to de house. Us cow-pen boys had to go drive up de caffs. Cow-pen boys? Cow-pen boys, dem de boys what keep away de caffs when dey do de milkin'. Co'se, lots of times when dey froo milkin', us jump on 'em and ride 'em. Wheneber dey ketch us doin' dat, dey sho' wear us out [gave us a spanking]. Dat warn't yestiddy [yesterday].

Fur as [As far as] I's concern, we had a plum [completely] good time in slav'ry. Many a year my grampa raise a bale of cotton and Marster buy it. Dat was encouragin' us to be smart.

Isaac Martin

My daddy name' Edmond Wood and my ma name' Maria. I had a brudder and a sister. Dey name' Cass and Ann. I been a farmer all my life. I kep' on farmin' 'til de boll weevil hit dese parts and den I quit de farm and went to public work. I work in de woods and cut logs. I buy dis house. I been here 'roun' Voth 'bout twenty-five year'.

I been marry twict. De fus' time I marry — I git so stinkin' ol' I can't 'member when it were, but it been a long ways back. My fus' wife Mary Johnson. She die' and den I marry dis yere woman I got yere now. Her name been Rhoda McGowan when I marry her, but she marry befo'. Bofe of us ol', ain't fit for nuttin'. Us git pension' and dat what us live on now 'cause I too ol' to do any work no mo'.

Me and my fus' wife we had ten chillun. Dey's all dead but fo' [four] and I ain't sho' dey's all livin'. Las' I heerd of 'em, one was in Houston, and one in Chicago, and one in Kansas City, and one live here. I see him dis mawnin'.

I heerd tell of de Klu Klux but I ain't neber seed 'em. I neber did go to school, needer.

I's a member of de C.M.E. Meth'dis' Chu'ch. When I uster could git about, I uster be a steward in de chu'ch. Den I was de treasurer of de chu'ch here at Voth for some seben year'. I uster b'long to de U.B.F. Lodge, too.

Back in slav'ry, dey allus had a ol' darky to train de young ones and teach 'em right from wrong. And dey'd whip you for doin' wrong. Dey'd repo't to de overseer. Some of 'em was mean and repo't somebody dey ain't like jis' to git 'em in trouble. De overseer he had to 'vestigate 'bout it and if it was so, somebody git a whippin'. Sometimes some folks repo't sump'n' when it warn't true.

Ol' Marster he was plum ind'pendant. His plantation was off from de town. He uster had his mail brung to him. Fur's I kin 'member, I didn' had to look out for nuttin'. Dey had a time to call all de slaves up and give 'em hats, and anudder time dey give 'em shoes, and anudder time dey give 'em clo's [clothes]. Dey see dat eb'rybody was fit. Ol' Marster allus give 'em all some kinder present at Crismus. I dunno what all he give de ol' folks, but he give de chillun candy and de like.

I was allus tickle' to see Ol' Marster come 'roun'. Oh, good gracious, yes. And it allus tickle' him to come 'roun' and see all his li'l niggers.

One time Cap'n Fisher was 'sociated wid Ol' Marster. Him and anudder man come 'long wid Ol' Marster up de road what run froo de quarters [through the area of the slave cabins]. Dey wanter see de li'l niggers. Ol' Marster call 'em up and frow out a han'ful of dimes. It sho' tickle' 'em to see de li'l niggers scramble for dem dimes. Us look' for dimes 'roun' dat place for a week. Dat was enjoyment to de white folks dem days.

Marster was good to his niggers and none of 'em eber run away. My mudder she raise Ol' Mistus' baby chile. She uster suckle [breastfeed] him jis' like he her own baby and he allus t'ink lots of her. After he a growed up man, he uster bring her presents lots of times. He call her Mammy all de time.

He went off to de war. He los' he hearin' and got deef [deaf]. Muster been de noise from dem big cannons what done it. He got his big toe shot off in de war, too. After de war was over, he come home and git married.

Dat 'bout all dat I kin 'member 'cep'n dat I vote' in de state and other 'lections when I's twenty-one year' ol'.

Slave mother and child (Names unknown)

LILY PERRY

I wus borned on de plantation of Mister Jerry Perry near Louisburg [North Carolina] about eighty-four years ago. My daddy, Riddick, 'longed ter him an' so did my mammy, 'do [although] she 'longed ter a Mis' Litchford 'fore she married daddy.

De fust things dat I can remember wus bein' a housegal, pickin' up chips [wood chips for use as kindling for the fire], mindin' de table, an' feedin' de hogs. De slop buckets [buckets of liquidy food mixture for the pigs] wus heavy an' I had a heap of wuck dat wus hard ter do. I done de very best dat I could, but often I got whupped jist de same.

When dey'd start ter whup me, I'd bite lak a run-mad dog. So, dey'd chain my han's. See hyar [here], hyar's de scars made by de chains. Dey'd also pick me up by de years [ears] an' fling me 'roun'. See hyar, I can wiggle my years up an' down, jist lak a mule can, an' I can wiggle 'em 'roun' an' 'roun' lak dat. See!

One day I ain't feelin' so good an' de slops am so heavy dat I stops an' pours out some of it. De oberseer, Zack Terrell, sees me an' when I gits back ter de house, he grabs me ter whup me.

De minute he grabs me, I seize on ter his thumb an' I bites hit [it] ter de bone. Den he gits mad an' he picks me up, an' lifts me higher dan my haid [head], an' flings me down on de steel mat dere in front of de do' [door].

Dey has ter revise [revive] me wid cold water from de spring. I wus sick for a week. We ain't had good food which makes me weak an' I still has ter do heavy wuck.

Dar wus a slave [auction] block in Louisburg an' I'se seed many a slave sold dar. Very few wus put in chains. Most of 'em wus put in a kivered wagon wid a guard an' wus chained at night. I'se seed many a 'oman cryin' fer her chile when one er de tother [one or the other] wus put on de slave block in Louisburg.

I wus 'bout twelve years old when de Yankees come. I wus pickin' up chips in de yard when dey comes by wid deir hosses steppin' high an' deir music playin' a happy chune. I wus skeered [scared], but I don't dasn't [dare not] run 'case Marster will sho' have me whupped. So, I keeps on wid my wuck.

Dey pass fast on down de road an' dey doan [don't] bother nothin' in our community, but de white folkses hates 'em jist de same.

Marster Jerry tells us 'bout a week later dat we am free. All of de two hundret, 'cept 'bout five or six, goes right off [leave the plantation]. He tells all of us dat he will pay us iffen we will stay an' wuck. So, me an' my family we stays on.

We lives dar fer seberal years. Den I marries Robert Perry who lives on de same plantation wid us. We ain't had but one daughter an' dat's Kats, who still libes wid me.

Me an' Robert wus raised up tergether, he bein' five years older'n me. I loved him from de time I wus borned. I know how he uster hate ter see me git dem beatin's an' he'd beg me not ter let my mouth be so sassy, but I can't help hit [it]. He uster take my beatin's when he could, an' a heap of times, he sneak out ter de fiel's in de evenin' an' toted [carried] dat slops ter de pigs.

Onct when Marster wus whuppin' me, Robert run up an' begged Marse ter put de whuppin' on him 'stead of me. De result wus Marse whupped us both an' we 'cided ter run away.

We did run away, but night brung us back ter another whuppin' an' we ain't never run away no mo'.

We wus at a frolic [party] at Louisburg [after Emancipation] when he proposes ter me an' he do hit dis way: "Honey Gal, I knows dat you doan [don't] love me so powerful much, but will you try ter do hit fer me?"

Course I sez, "Go 'long, nigger. Iffen I doan love yo' den dar ain't no water in Tar Riber." Den I sez, "We can git Marse Henry outen de bed an' he'll marry us ternight."

Rob was tickled pink an', sho' 'nuff [sure enough], we wus married right away dat very night.

We lived pore [poor], dat I knows, but we wus too happy in ourselves ter worry 'bout sich things an' de lak.

I laughs now ter think how ignorant we niggers wus. We'd do our washin' an' 'bout de time we hung hit on de line, we'd see a string of folks comin' home from de Prospect Church an' we'd know dat we'd done our washin' on a Sunday.

The I WAS A SLAVE Book Collection
SUBTITLES OF BOOKS

EACH SUBTITLE IS <u>ONE SEPARATELY PUBLISHED</u> BOOK:

AVAILABLE NOW:
- Book 1: Descriptions of Plantation Life
- Book 2: The Lives of Slave Men
- Book 3: The Lives of Slave Women
- Book 4: The Breeding of Slaves
- Book 5: The Lives of Slave Children

UPCOMING BOOKS (being published in this order, one at a time*)
- Book 6: Slave Auctions
- Book 7: The Bullwhip and Other Treatments
- Book 8: Runaways and Resistances
- Book 9: Field and House Slaves
- Book 10: How Plantations Operated
- Book 11: Literacy and Unusual Circumstances
- Book 12: Slaveowners: Hated and Loved
- Book 13: Mulatto Slaves: Slave Mother and White Father
- Book 14: City, Frontier, and Riverboat Slaves
- Book 15: Slave Families and Separations
- Book 16: Patrollers and the Ku Klux Klan
- Book 17: The Lives of Slaveowners
- Book 18: Remembering Africans and Indians
- Book 19: Religion, Songs, and Communications
- Book 20: The Civil War: What the Slaves Saw and Did
- Book 21: Freedom!!!
- Book 22: The Lives of Ex-Slaves: 1865-1937
- Book 23: Plantation Days Remembered
- Book 24: Superstitions, Ghost Stories, and Great Quotes

••••••••• **PLEASE NOTICE** •••••••••

At the time of the printing of this book, **only the first five books were available.** Please do not order unpublished books in advance. Please call 202-737-7827 to learn if additional books are available.

(*When you order by mail, you are placed on our mailing list and will receive a postcard when each new book is published. There are no set publication times.)

ORDERING INFORMATION

Please look on page 63 for a list of available books.

PLEASE DO NOT ORDER BOOKS
THAT HAVE NOT BEEN PUBLISHED YET.

> **TO ORDER BY MAIL:**
> **$9.50 for any one book**
> plus $8.50 for each additional book mailed at the same time
> *(Prices include postage and handling)*
> Example: Five books total $43.50

Mail your *printed* name and address with ZIP code,
(telephone numbers are optional, but should be included, just in case)
along with the **subtitles of each book** ordered,
quantities of each book, and your check or money order to:

American Legacy Books
P.O. Box 1393-B
Washington, DC 20013

To mail Discover, MasterCard, VISA, or American Express orders,
purchasers MUST include
(1) credit card number (2) expiration date,
(3) telephone number (a requirement), and (4) SIGNATURE.

Credit card orders by fax: 202-546-1919 must include **all** of above.

Current ordering information and publication dates
can be accessed on-line: **www.iwasaslave.com**
or call
202-737-7827
Automated information: 24 hours
Customer service: Monday-Friday, 9:00-5:00 Eastern time
for information and for placement of credit card orders

IMPORTANT: **At the time that this book was printed, only 1 through 5 were available.** Call to learn if more books have been published: 202-737-7827 — OR — for a free brochure listing all currently available books *(and price increases, if any, since this book was published)*, please <u>send a self-addressed and stamped envelope</u> to the above address.